And
Crown
Thy
Good

A Yachats Book of Faith and Action

Dr Karl C Evans

Dedication

This book is dedicated with thanks to the many people of the counties I visited. Without their wisdom and their willingness to speak openly with a stranger, I simply could not have done my work. God bless all of you.

I also have deep gratitude toward Dr. Doug Johnson and the rest of the National Division of the General Board of Global Ministries. You put me in a position to do this work, knowing that the final product would be critical of the operation of the Board and of the entire Church. Such commitment to honesty and service makes mission possible.

Thank you.
Karl

ISBN:1453651691
EAN:9781453651698

Contents

Foreword

In 1987 Dr. Douglas Johnson of the General Board of Global Ministries invited the author to prepare for and participate in a study of the twenty-five counties in the United States that showed the lowest per capita income for 1986.

Over the next two months, I visited two or three of these counties to discover appropriate questions and directions of study. I then wrote up the general directions of the study, and a small group of us scattered to the remaining counties to discover what we could.

The specific issue involved in the study was whether the General Board of Global Ministries had any possibility of making a positive economic impact in the counties involved, and what might that process or impact look like.

Additionally, if any substantial good is to be done, what would it cost in finances and personnel? At that point we were not thinking of any cost that might arise in social status, organizational stability or self esteem for the workers.

Approximately six months later, the entire group gathered at Oklahoma City to make our final report. Some of the matters and issues reported by the group were quite expected, others were quite unbelievable. The final result, of course, was that a line or two was added to the Mission Statement of the National Division. Effectively, as well, the project appears to have had little impact on these particular counties.

At that meeting, I asked Dr. Johnson if I might write my own book on the subject. I was concerned that the report itself might never really see the light of day.

He laughed and gave his assent quite willingly, probably also suspecting nothing would come of his project. He seemed to be quite disappointed with what we had learned.

Now, years later, with neither the Church nor the community having done anything much to implement anything from the study, it is my turn.

There is a quick answer to the questions of the study. Yes, the General Board of Global Ministries as well as all the local congregations not only of the United Methodist Church but all faith groups could, if they would, have enormous impact on these communities. The cost would be amazingly small in finances and personnel, and the nature of the impact would shape the life of the Church in the United States for decades to come.

However, there is a very human characteristic that keeps such support from happening in the churches. That characteristic is the enormity of the expensive hierarchy of the churches, including the United Methodist Church, the Roman Catholic Church, the Southern Baptist Church, the Church of Jesus Christ of Latter Day Saints, and all the rest.

Before getting into what can be done by the denomination in the mission field of rural poverty, we should take a look at the realities of need.

And Crown Thy Good...

The United States has been known around the world as the "Land of Opportunity". It is as if this were our national motto.

Yet within this land several hundred communities struggle for generations, even centuries, to break out of the bonds of poverty that hold them. Perhaps the most grinding poverty in the U.S. is seen in the rural counties involved in this study. In some of these counties, even the wealthiest of persons have only modest means. In all of them, death from malnutrition including starvation is said to be not uncommon. The difficulty is in proving it without the assistance of the federal government.

Perhaps the most precious role of the federal government in these counties would be to simply document what is happening. Then a variety of organizations and institutions (including the federal government itself) might be convinced to help with the recovery.

However, recent directions of government operations have tended to shift moneys away from those populations and projects that need the most assistance. Instead, the moneys are seemingly directed into the pockets of the Washington politicians and Fortune 500 CEO's at the expense of the poorest of the poor.

It is important to note that the lowest fifty or so counties on the scale of per capita income tend to bounce around a little in their ratings. The particular list of counties of this study, for instance, might have been quite a different lot if the study had been done a year later or earlier.

However, I am convinced the counties visited are not exceptional. Rather, they seem to accurately portray poverty in rural America.

We should also note that local issues and realities can and do change quite rapidly. If you happen to be in one of these counties and find things not exactly as I call them, do not be disappointed. Only celebrate that the human situation can and does change quite often. Without that there would be no hope.

These counties were selected by Dr. Johnson from data in the County and State Data Book. Later issues of the book will give different information about the ranking of these counties, and their various demographic and economic numbers. The serious student of economic development will want to compare the data used here with prior and later data.

I am convinced, however, that these counties are representative enough of rural poverty in America that little will be added in general knowledge of the situation.

The reader should also know that this book is not written in order to impress anyone with the depth of poverty in these counties. That is easily enough done.

What is more difficult is to find areas of change and support that might build a basis of economic growth for these people. Hope is needed, a heavier picture of despair is not.

Let us find what we can do rather than revel in the sorry plight of humanity. It may well be that the greatest weakness of capitalism is that it allows us to compete, even psychologically, with persons who have no means to compete. Then those with the wealth feel so good!

The Counties

Arizona:	Apache County	St. Johns
Utah:	San Juan County	Monticello
Colorado:	Conejos County	Conejos
New Mexico:	Mora County	Mora
Texas:	Maverick County	Eagle Pass
	Starr County	Rio Grande City
	Zavala County	Crystal City
Arkansas:	Lee County	Marianna
Mississippi:	Jefferson County	Fayette
	Tunica County	Tunica
Tennessee:	Hancock County	Sneedville
Kentucky:	Elliott County	Sandy Hook
	McCreary County	Whitley City
	Owsley County	Booneville
South Dakota:	Buffalo County	
	Corson County	Gann Valley
	Dewey County	Timberlake
	Douglas County	Armour
	Harding County	Buffalo
	Mellette County	White River
	Shannon County	Pine Ridge
	Todd County	Mission
	Ziebach County	Dupree
North Dakota:	Sioux County	Fort Yates
Montana:	Petroleum County	Winnett

Native American

Of the original twenty five counties in the project, about one third, (eight) are primarily Native American in population. If we had included the various regions of Alaska as well, the ratio would have been significantly higher.

There seems to be one primary factor in this preponderance of Native Americans in the list of the poorest of the poor in the land. That is, that these people have suffered both from the invaders' (the rest of us) unwillingness to include them in the social, cultural, political, economic and spiritual fabric of the nation, and from their own resistance to being included.

One Navajo at Chinle told me "Every day I get up in the morning and curse the White Man for taking my birthright from me. Every night I curse myself for trying to work my way back into that birthright by acting like a White Man."

The Native Americans in this study are actually of two separate and quite distinct cultures. The Navajo and Zuni of Apache County, Arizona, are primarily a settled and agrarian population. They have been this since their entry into the area a millenium ago.

The Sioux of the northern plains, on the other hand, have never willingly been farmers. Historically, they have migrated with the buffalo herds across the waves of prairie grass. Today, even when there is a small patch of tillable soil in the rocky patches designated as reservations, some tell me they have difficulty seeing themselves as farmers. Thus crops may be poorly tended should any attempt be made at agriculture.

With the absolutely horrible conditions of the soil of most of the reservations in the U.S., this cultural resistance can only result in massive poverty. It would be most difficult to grow a crop on most of the reservation land, and an unwillingness to try simply makes matters worse.

I was not fortunate enough to visit any of the northern plains counties among the twenty five. Other workers did that. I did, however, visit a large part of the Navajo, Hopi, Zuni and Apache lands.

It was only in these areas that I found it difficult to obtain information from local people. In other areas it was sometimes impossible to squeeze the information out of official sources. However, I could always count on going to a local tavern, or a church, or down by the town square on a Saturday night, and getting what I needed. People seemed to want to talk.

But the residents did not want to talk in San Juan or Apache Counties. This was not just the Native Americans who wanted to clam up. Both these counties are split, Anglo and Native American. Both have strong Mormon populations.

It took me much longer to find persons who would reveal the nature of the struggles within. I have come to the conclusion that one of the problems is that the Reservation structure, including the Bureau of Indian Affairs, is so counter to the nature of God's World, of being human, that it causes humans to operate in very unnatural ways. Additionally, the distrust of the Mormon power thrust is seen as an affront to the others.

People do not talk to each other. People do not work together. People, even people of good will, do not purchase goods from or sell goods to each other. In these senses, it is very akin to slavery.

Both these counties had the highest levels of both personal and institutional racism I found anywhere in the study. Apache County is actually two counties, separate and alienated. Given the power, those two might separate from each other formally and both be calmer.

On the other hand, there is both power and prestige for two sets of politicians by keeping the county together. They get to run for office, sit on committees and commissions and file papers with official jurisdictions all over the place. The Anglo politicians get to impress the Navajo and Zuni people. The Navajo and Zuni bigshots can do the same with the Anglo population.

There is a certain ego trip in being officially a part of two different worlds. For that reason, I suspect it will never change until the Navajo population forces it. That is a long way off.

Geography

Apache County lies along the northern portion of the boundary between Arizona and New Mexico. It is a county of rolling hills, deep canyons, and high mesas. With an area of 11,211 square miles, Apache county is larger than several states.

The northern half of the county is taken up by a portion of the Navajo Nation Reservation. This reservation occupies about one-sixth of the total land area of Arizona, plus a major portion of New Mexico and a piece of Utah. In the center of the Navajo Reservation is the land set aside for the Hopi Nation, nearly 3500 square miles. This land is not in Apache County.

The Navajo land in Apache County is rough land in that water is quite scarce. However it should not be assumed that the land is non-farmable. Much of the land would raise a variety of crops were water available. It is unlikely that water for the land would ever be available from the Colorado river because of the demands by the urban areas of Arizona and California. In fact, the City of Phoenix and other Arizona cities are buying up Arizona farmland at a prodigious rate in order to return the land to desert and provide water rights for further metropolitan development.

Some water is available and being used on the Navajo nation. This water, mostly from deep wells but some also from small streams, is limited and quite expensive. Most of the water is used in the support of the human population and the minimal livestock industry in the county. The county has only 10,000 total acres of crop land, nearly all of it in hay and grain.

Two other areas of the county are reservation. There is a small Zuni Reservation, of about 30 square miles just outside St. Johns, and the Fort Apache Reservation includes about 700 square miles in the southwest corner of the county.

The Fort Apache Reservation is primarily a high forested area. The land rises to a high point at Baldy Peak at 11,590 feet above sea level. The forests are largely dry pine areas with some other species filling in. These forests, because of the dry climate and the elevation, do not reproduce quickly, but the various agencies involved are becoming more adept at conservation and propagation measures. The Sitgreaves National Forest includes land surrounding the Reservation in Apache County. The national forest land is on the Mogollon Rim which extends about 150 miles west to east across Arizona.

Along the west central border of the county sets the Petrified Forest National Park. This National Park of about 150 square miles straddles Interstate 40 just inside the Apache County line. It is perhaps the premier exhibit of petrified wood in North America. Many local residents and officials are attempting to strengthen the impact of both the living forests and the petrified forests on the economy of Apache County, but federal priorities have severely limited this prospect.

The open land in the center of the county, from Springerville to Chambers, is farmed in a few places. For the most part it is useful only for raising antelope and rabbits. Cattle grazing is quite limited because of the real lack of vegetation. In much of this land there is simply no possibility of cattle grazing. In other areas some grazing is practiced.

History

The history of Apache County is a history of people fighting over land that is as inhospitable as any land in the country. Most of the important history is tied up in two areas, the Navajo Reservation and the area around St. John.

The Navajo are not the first civilization to inhabit the Four Corners area of Arizona, New Mexico, Colorado, and Utah. Other ancient peoples, including the Hopis, have attempted to make this vast area home. Some have been more successful at it than others. The remains of their civilizations are scattered across the area.

The establishment of Tseghahodzani (Window Rock) as the administration center for the Navajo Nation Reservation came in the 1930's. The Navajo Nation and the Bureau of Indian Affairs share a niche in the cliff. The town of Window Rock has major four-lane highways through it and in the direction of other cities in the area. A new major shopping center highlights the area.

The Navajo and Hopi people (and the Navajo in Apache County) happened to have been in the area as technologies have developed which promise to make the land much more hospitable. Drilling deep wells for water brought up with electric power, traveling the huge distances in air conditioned vehicles, communicating by radio and television and telephone, eating canned or refrigerated food, and operating huge strip-mine machinery to take the coal from the ground are making it possible to be comfortable and cosmopolitan in a harsh land.

The transition has not come easily. Virginia Daniels, Assistant Director of Development for the Navajo Nation, noted that the Navajos have historically resisted commercial and industrial development at the same time they have wished for its advantages. Now the Nation is coming to find ways of development that both give the advantages hoped for and provide protection for many of the old ways and traditions of the people.

The Zuni and Apache and Hopi face the same issues, although not on so large a scale as the Navajo people. All these groups have begun to participate in economic development in a variety of ways.

The nature of the relationship between the Native Americans and the surrounding governmental entities has become increasingly complex. For instance, the State of Arizona does not tax Indian lands and Indian owned property on reservations. Incomes of Indians residing on reservations are not taxed by the state if wholly derived from reservation sources. The Federal Government does not exempt individual Indians from income or other taxes. Indian people of Arizona are also exempt from state and local taxes on consumer goods purchased on the reservation, unless such taxes are imposed by the tribal government. Arizona does tax the property and business transactions of non Indians who operate on reservations and Indians who live or work off reservations.

Much tension arises within the county over this entire system of taxation. The county is responsible for providing certain services to the reservation. Another part of the tension here is that certain parts of the reservation which are within the county are over 200 miles from the county seat, and the county must operate outpost courthouses for the convenience of the persons who live in that area.

The area around St. John has an entirely different history and culture. This area was settled in the late 1600's by several persons of Spanish origin who moved in among the resident native population. The community remained small, and eventually the non-European population moved either south or north.

In 1879 Mormon settlers came to the area and found a thriving agricultural community built around the marshy lands along the streams. They built their strength, and today the Mormon population is the power structure of the community. The Stake Center (church) is separated from the county court house by only a few inches and largely indistinguishable from it both in location and in power.

In recent years several Protestant groups have begun to appear in various communities in Apache County, but none currently have the impact of the Mormon community in the political structure of the Anglo community.

Population

Seventy-five percent of the population of Apache County is Native American and four percent are Spanish Origin. Most of the Native Americans reside on the Navajo Reservation, although about five thousand live either on the other reservations or in the non-reservation communities.

With less than five persons per square mile over the entire county, the area could house many more persons. That is unlikely in the foreseeable future because of the non-existence of water supplies.

The county has one of the highest birth rates in the nation, at 31.6 births per thousand residents per year. The nation averages 15.9, and Arizona as a whole averages 15.6.

The marriage rate is 3.2 per thousand compared with the nation's 10.6, and the divorce rate is 0.4 compared with the nations's 5.2. The serious crime rate is about one fifth that of the national average. Various theories are put forth for these divergences from the state and national averages. No one theory seems to cover all the bases. The Navajo Nation operates its own Bureau of Data and Statistics which investigates these matters on the reservation.

Fred Yazzi, United Methodist Pastor at Shiprock, New Mexico, and part of the Four Corners Ministry, says that the Native Americans are really just beginning to learn how to live in the contemporary world, and that this transition leaves some people behind for a while, and eventually they will catch up. Of course, there are some ways in which he hopes the Navajo never catch up to the Anglo.

A significant factor in Navajo County is that only 4% of the workers in the county are self-employed, compared with 7% in the United States and 6% in Arizona. One of the difficulties is certainly that of language, for unlike Hispanics, various Native American groups do not have a truly common language base and population understanding.

Mr. Yazzi commented that one of the great difficulties between the Indian and the Anglo is in the use of the legal system. In discussions of the ownership and use of land, for instance, English Civil Law recognizes land as property, completely divorced from the personality or personhood of the owner. Land can readily be sold, traded, swapped, mined, stolen, or any number of other events without personal impact on the owner or resident.

Indian culture and tradition, on the other hand, treat the land as a real extension of the personhood of the owner or resident. If the land is flooded, the resident is being attacked. If the land is sold, the resident loses a part of one's personality. If the land is mined, a scar is opened in the relationship between the resident and the land.

This issue reaches its toughest point when land agents approach the Indian about acquiring land. Railroad right of way purchasers, or mining company representatives, or timber company representatives, or government agents, or utilities developers all do this. Because of language difficulties, and having had a history of being pushed around the continent these past 400 years, the Indian probably will understand there is no recourse but to accept the proposal.

The Indian may well not have understand that bartering is expected, for in some Indian groups bartering or dickering is simply not acceptable. In any case the deal will probably be signed on the terms of the purchaser. <u>In the process the Indian has not only lost the land, at an unfair price, but has known all along that a part of the process is a personal attack on the seller which the seller has to accept.</u>

Yazzi says the younger Navajo are coming to understand this system and are prepared to barter and dicker and argue, but many older persons find this to be both demeaning and futile.

Yazzi says that the younger people are beginning to see that competition is the root of racism, and that to combat racism, one has to compete for the higher jobs, the higher positions, the more lucrative careers. This new awakening requires a self esteem that the Indian people have not expressed in centuries.

Part of this need for self esteem expression is being met by the development of National Newspaper, the <u>Navajo Times</u> and a Navajo Language radio station, broadcasting from Window Rock. Although both of these have been caught in problems of the newly redeveloping political system of the Navajos, both should have a strong influence on the future success of the reservation.

For some time there has been discussion of the possibility of dividing the county. The discussion has taken many forms, not all of which have high motives. If the Navajo Nation can continue to develop its economy, that move might not be pressed so closely by the Anglo population. The potential development of the portion of the reservation that lies within Arizona as a county might be considered at a later date. The same might be true of the other reservation areas of the state as well.

Economy

Fifty four percent of the employment in Apache County is government service. City, county, state, national, and tribal governments employ over half the working population of Apache County. There is an unemployment ratio of 75% among the Navajo, and a ratio of 43% among the Zuni. The two peoples account for 85% of the population of the county. With an overall unemployment rate in the county of 26%, it appears almost every non-Indian in the county who wishes to work has a job of some kind.

The primary heavy industry in the county consists of a pulpwood mill and a coal fired electric generation plant, both in the St. John area. The around the clock nature of these operations requires a large work force basically recruited from local workers. Because of the distances, few Navajo or Apache workers are part of the crew.

Some coal reserves are a part of the Navajo land, and have been mined to some extent. However, for the reasons discussed above, this has not been pursued with much vigor until just the last few years. As the Navajo nation becomes more complex and more adept at economic development, it might be expected that these operations will be expanded.

The Navajo Nation has pressed ahead with the development of high tech industries such as computer microchip production. Some operations of this type have begun, and with good success. The traditional values of patience, hand work, formed beauty, and personal relationships with the created object are assets in this work.

Later economic development in Apache County likely will take the form of some tourism, some manufacturing, and considerable entrepreneurship in hand work.

Church

Apache County is a bewildering array of competing and widely divergent religious groups. The Mormon community is the primary Anglo group, although the Roman Catholic faith has not been shunted completely aside. Because the Roman Catholic congregation began as a Spanish Mission, and the community was primarily Spanish until the end of the 19th century, the congregation was not heavily populated with Anglos until recently.

Because the Mormon community quickly became involved in marketing and in governmental affairs, the county became a stronghold Mormon community. However, in the last few years, a number of other denominations (including United Methodist) have established congregations in the southern half of Apache County. Assemblies of God, Baptist, Church of Christ, and others have begun to recognize the potential of this area.

The Reservation is a different story. In 1940, there were 30 Christian congregations in all of the Reservation, including portions in New Mexico, Colorado, and Utah. Today there are over 300, and nearly a dozen of these are United Methodist.

The United Methodist Church has a spotty record at best in support of these communities. It has obviously been involved in a variety of ways. A new congregation has been set up in Apache County within the last year to go with the congregation already working at Window Rock. The Navajo congregations at Tselina and Window Rock are part of the New Mexico Annual Conference and the Four Corners ministry.

The Four Corners Ministry is centered in Shiprock, New Mexico, and serves a large area of four states. Paul West and Fred Yazzi oversee a substantial and un-conventional program of Anglo and Native American ministries. The small congregation at Window Rock plays only a small role in community affairs, but is nonetheless important as a United Methodist presence in the center of Navajo culture. The new congregation at Tselani, near Chinle, is both needed for growth and as a sign of a developing ministry for the Navajo People.

Congregational development among reservation peoples is quite different for a variety of reasons. Any land must be leased rather than purchased, for it is all federal land in trust. Traditional roles for church officers such as trustees and lay leaders don't always fit the culture. Even some of the more intentionally planned moves can work backwards to the need if they violate cultural sensitivities.

However, in the face of this, the Four Corners Ministry moves on, doing its work. I have appreciated the years I have known Fred Yazzi and been aware of the problems faced by the Four Corners Ministry. He deals with a large number of alcoholics in his work. Even as we visited he was called by one of his members for some words on dealing with personal struggles with Alcohol. There is a strong support for Alcoholics Anonymous in the ministry there.

<u>General</u>

Sitting at the picnic shelter at the Navajo Nation Zoological park having lunch, I became tired enough that I put my head down and took a little nap. When I woke a few minutes later, it took me several seconds to remember where I was. The traffic, children playing, voices arguing about Irangate, were the same. Yet I was in the heart of the "hardest land in America," and among the forgotten people.

I finally sat up, listening, drinking my Dr. Pepper, eating a tuna sandwich, watching people, enjoying the sun and the clear day, wondering about the business at the very large and modern shopping center across the busy highway. I have sat like that, waiting for appointments, at a thousand cities across America.

I went over to the sandstone cliff, hoping to find signs of an ancient civilization that might have passed through here. I was not disappointed except in the time line. The hieroglyphics were there. "Ed + Mary 1984" "Dodge City Rebels" "I LUV NY" "This ain't Kansas."

And one other slight difference. I turned to watching Old Glory waving in the breeze, and saw also the golden flag of the Navajo Nation.

Apache, Arizona   Trend Information

Population and Households

	1970	1980	% Chg	1986	% Chg	1991	% Chg
	Census	Census	70-80	(Est.)	80-86	(Proj.)	86-91
Population	32298	52108	61.3	54806	5.2	56962	3.9
Households	6832	12638	85.0	13671	8.2	14583	6.7
Household Size	4.65*	4.09	-12.0	3.98	-2.7	3.88	-2.5
Group Quarters	408	408	0.0	408	0.0		
	1969	1979	% Chg	1986	% Chg	1991	%Chg
Income	Census	Census	69-79	Est.	79-86	Proj	86-91
Agg. Income($mm)	41.4	173.9	320.1	259.9	49.4	321.5	23.7
Per Capita ($)	1282	3338	160.4	4743	42.1	5644	19.0
Average Hh ($)	5983	13693	128.9	18859	37.7	21873	16.0
Median Hh ($)	5544	11394	105.5	15299	34.3	18115	18.4
Household	Income	Distribution					
	1979		1986		1991		
	Count	%	Count	%	Count	%	
Less than $7,500	4619	36.5	3581	26.2	3267	22.4	
$ 7,500 - $14,999	3274	25.9	3170	23.2	3110	21.3	
$15,000 - $24,999	2661	21.1	2825	20.7	2936	20.1	
$25,000 - $34,999	1382	10.9	1905	13.9	2050	14.1	
$35,000 - $49,999	549	4.3	1531	11.2	1914	13.1	
$50,000 - $74,999	132	1.0	535	3.9	995	6.8	
$75,000 and over	21	0.2	124	0.9	311	2.1	

*1970 Household Size Is an Estimate Based on 1970 Census Data.
Data on Income Are Expressed in "Current" Dollars for Each Respective Year.
Hh=household   Agg=aggregate

San Juan, Utah
County Seat: Monticello

San Juan County covers 7725 square miles of southeastern Utah. Approximately one fourth of the county and one third of the population is within the bounds of the Navajo Reservation. San Juan County, as are all the areas of the Rio Grande and Colorado River drainage, has a history of well over 10,000 years of settlement. San Juan County has had European heritage settlers since about 1650.

This land is not generally recognized as being fertile, yet some of the land produces good crops of wheat and beans. Even some of the least fertile land can support a few head of sheep and goats. The various native populations over the last several thousand years have been able to flourish through a combination of hard work, patience, wisdom, and perhaps a miracle now and then.

Geography

The upper Colorado River and Lake Powell provide most of the western and northern borders of the county. This majestic stream flowing through the Canyonlands National Park continues through the Grand Canyon and down to the Gulf of California. The Green River coming from the north joins the Colorado thirty miles northwest of Monticello and forms a short portion of the boundary.

A line drawn east to west about five miles south of Moab from the Green River to the Colorado border forms the rest of the northern boundary. From there the boundary runs south on the Colorado state line and west along the Arizona state line. San Juan County touches New Mexico at the Four Corners monument, the only point in the nation where four states come together.

Two areas of the county are included in national forests. The Manti-La Sal National Forest is divide into two sections, along the northern border and near the center of the county. These forested areas do not produce a large amount of timber although some good pine stands are common. Most of the area in both instances is brushy cover more suited as game habitat than for timber.

The southern section of the Manti-La Sal National Forest includes the Abajo Mountains just west of Monticello. This small range provides potential for recreational use, water supply and some potential for timber. At a maximum 11,019 feet, this range commands the surrounding countryside.

The southern portion of the county is one of the most photographed areas of the nation. This hauntingly beautiful area appears regularly in various periodicals showing its natural beauty, the hardiness of its people and the difficulty of its economy.

The San Juan River runs from east to west along the southern end of the county, joining the Colorado River thirty miles northeast of Page, Arizona. This river is one of the great marvels of the world. For thousands of years it has eaten its way into the soft soil of the Four Corners country, creating massive canyons, towering cliffs, and starting billions of tons of topsoil on its way to the Gulf of California.

The river is not the only erosive force in the area. The steady wind has blown sand against the faces of nature presented in the area and created pillars, surrealistic shapes and bare rock fields in the process.

The beauty of this land may have contributed heavily to the Navajo and Ute concepts of the sacredness of the land itself. In the Monument Valley the shapes seem to be calling one to experience a different reality itself.

Some farming is taken up along the Colorado border. Small communities pop up here and there with a few facilities, a few homes, and oh, yes, some oil wells. In addition some areas of the county have a relatively good supply of uranium ore.

For the most part, the land in the southern half of the county is only slightly productive. Much of the land is rock surface with no potential of growing any vegetation. Other portions have some bits of grass and brush here and there, but only along the rivers and streams can one find any real attempts to cultivate crops.

History

San Juan County history is as varied and colorful as any in the world. It is a history of wars and settlements and exploration and myth. It is a history of Europeans and native populations and religious causes and persecution. The populations have come into the area for a variety of reasons. Some have come after gold or other minerals. Some have come in a quest for land--any land. Some have come out of religious persecution, and some have come to persecute religiously.

The Anasazi (the Ancient Ones) were in the area from around 12,000 BC that we know of. There may have been earlier settlers. These people lived in homes dug from or built into the cliffs along the rivers, and in homes made of travertine, logs, and mud in other areas. Travertine is laid down by geological process and is abundant in the area. It is easily broken into brick-like chunks and used as building blocks. The various clays and muds in the area make good sealers and mortar for the travertine.

The use of travertine in buildings has enabled us to become very familiar with the life styles of the Anasazi of the area. The area is as famous for its ruins as for its unforgiving soil. Many of the ruins have been rebuilt for our enjoyment and education. The Edge of the Cedar ruins at Blanding are perhaps the easiest to visit, although they are not the most impressive.

Following the disappearance of the Anasazi civilization various peoples of the plains and the coasts began to come into the areas. The reasons for this migration are unclear, although simple population pressures and military economies may have played large roles.

The Navajo people came into the area around 800 AD bringing with them their Athabascan related language and a willingness to work with the land rather than against it. For the Navajo of today, the land is really quite personal. It can be both supporter and enemy. Even in the best of times there is little room for laughter for tough times are coming again. Navajo culture is one of the most intentionally forward looking cultures of the world. One does not live in this land for 600 years by operating without very specific planning.

In the middle 16th century the Spaniards began to explore the entire area of the Great Basin as well as these rivers that at times seemed so foreboding. The gold and other precious metal they found was not enough to satisfy their lust, but was enough to convince others that more bright metal was to be found.

In the early 1800's Kit Carson came into the area and attempted to drive the Navajo from the rivers where he believed the gold to be. He destroyed their homes and forced them into yet another "Long Walk". Some managed to escape and return their land. It is thought that several of these were able to form a small community in the area of Mexican Hat.

During these years a variety of settlers were coming into the area from various parts of the world. Some were coming into the northern portions of the county, finding the better soil more attractive than a continued search for California and gold. Some were coming only from Colorado. Some were moving up from the Spanish settlements along the Rio Grande in New Mexico, Texas, and Old Mexico.

When the Mormons began to arrive in the area in 1880 they found a flourishing culture in the northern county. Many of these Mormons had been in groups originally sent to colonize Old Mexico. Rebuffed south of the Rio Grande, these people returned to Utah to join with another band in San Juan County. Although they failed to totally dislodge the incumbent community, they did become the dominant culture in the northern sections of the county.

The Mormons were able to achieve this for two reasons. First, the other European settlers who had come earlier had stretched to the breaking point their supply and reinforcement routes with their native lands. Spain was in decline and could not provide support. Mexico would have liked to have been deeply involved this far north but it did not have the civil strength to put together a decisive movement.

Second, the Mormons were already established at Salt Lake City and were moving out <u>a community at a time</u> to take control of surrounding areas. Several families at a time were sent out at once from a central authority. This factor gave immediate strength to an otherwise frustrating project. Their supply lines were relatively short. When the line was threatened, the group was simply pulled back to a manageable distance. Non-Mormon settlers in the area were there mostly as single family units without organizational support.

When the original Navajo Reservation was formed in 1884, the seeds were sown for racial separation. Some say enforced poverty also was the result. Until recent years the Navajo people have not been a part of any monetary economy within the county.

More recently, numbers of Navajos and members of other tribes and nations, particularly the Utes, have made homes in Monticello and Blanding. In times of good prosperity there have been jobs for these people, although some suggest that in tough times these are the first workers laid off.

Population

Demographically, San Juan County is typical of many counties of the Intermountain West with a majority of Anglo residents, a large minority of Native Americans, and a small number of Hispanic residents. Most of the Hispanic residents came here originally for military duty or to perform agricultural labor. Some are remnants of Spanish settlers from two centuries ago. In San Juan County only about 4% are Hispanic. Nearly half are Native American.

As with a number of the counties in this study, there are more males than females in the county. Local residents attribute this the extreme difficulty a single woman has in finding employment. There are precious few jobs for women in San Juan County.

The emphases of the Latter Day Saints (Mormons) and some affects of poverty among the Native Americans are typically given as the reasons that households in the county average 4.14 persons. This is significantly higher than the national average of 2.75 and the state average of 3.2.

Drastically lower rates of marriage and divorce are seen as the result of two factors. First, the 35% or so Mormon population typically prefer to have their wedding in a Temple, and there is no Mormon Temple in San Juan County. Couples take their weddings (and thus their money) to one of the various temples in other areas of Utah.

Second, many of the divorces of county population actually take place in some other area. With so little possibility of a job in the county, a woman leaving her husband will typically move to Salt Lake City or some other urban area before filing for divorce. Over half the female householder families in San Juan County are living below the poverty level compared to 28% in the state.

Although official unemployment statistics for San Juan County show a rate of about 10% at this time, most social services personnel in the area argue for a considerably larger rate. Reservation residents are not counted in the official statistics for the county. Very few women in the county bother to look for work both because there is little available and there is a built-in bias against working women.

When the President of the Church of Jesus Christ of Latter Day Saints (Mormon) called on the women of the Church to quit their jobs and turn the work over to men, at least three women in the county did so. Several other women left jobs at about that time, but it is not clear that they did so because of the request of the Church.

Economy

Employment in San Juan County is concentrated in the mining and government sectors. In June 1986, San Juan County had a civilian labor force of 3,650 and was supporting 2.940 non-agricultural wage and salary jobs. Just under one-third the labor force is Native American. The unofficial unemployment figure for Native Americans in the county is 17%, although most local authorities state a figure close to 60% including those who would apply for work if they felt a job was likely to be available.

Over the past ten years the average pay rate for non-agricultural jobs has been higher than the state average. This can be traced to an increase in government jobs, employment in oil, and very high wages in uranium mining and processing. The oil and uranium employment is now shrinking although the wage rates are still quite high. Local expectation is that uranium mining and processing will temporarily end in December 1987.

From 1984 to 1986 per capita income dropped from $6,000 to $4,484. Most of this decline is traceable to the decline in the numbers of jobs in the county.

San Juan County has a variety of natural resources including oil, gas, uranium, silver, gold and vanadium. The county is the state's leading producer of oil and gas. The Greater Aneth oil field, in the extreme southeast of the county, has produced more oil than any other oil field in Utah. The Lisbon Field is the state's largest natural gas field. There are currently five gas processing plants located in San Juan County.

The complete shutdown of one major industry, the decline of others, and the rapid mechanization of another have left the county with a surplus of both workers and housing. Residences are selling at prices far less than half the price those same residences would bring in Salt Lake City.

The major industry that has shut down totally was the test firing of the Pershing Missiles. This process brought several hundred military and civilian personnel to the area during the 1970's. When this process was complete, those persons either left town or stayed on to work in the uranium industry. Now that industry is about gone as well. Those workers must now find work in other areas.

Just prior to the rise of the missile industry, the pinto bean industry had undergone major mechanization. Although the beans had been generally harvested by machine for some time, rapid improvement in machinery and processing added still further to the surplus of unskilled labor in the community.

The shrinkage of population in Blanding and Monticello has left the two cities with a surplus of available utilities and services. Good water and sewer services now in existence will probably not need additions for some time to come.

The quality of life in San Juan County is surprisingly good. Two hospitals, county-wide school system, a county road system that does provide nearly all the road work for the portion of the reservation within the county, and immediate access to several National Parks and National Monuments truly make this one of the more attractive areas for living and visiting.

Two major industries that should spring to the surface in the county over the next few years are retirement and tourism.

With a good climate, four complete seasons, good services, inexpensive housing and utilities, San Juan County should become more attractive to retirees as Arizona continues to lose its luster as retirement Mecca.

San Juan County lies squarely at the crossroads of major tourist movement. It is on the primary route from Texas to the Northwest, and from north central states to Arizona and California. Tourist services are slowly building but there is still need for a variety of services in the county.

The State of Utah and the federal government both have plans to work in the area to increase tourist activities. Added scenic overlooks, especially along the highways, will be of significant value. More prominent invitational signs are also planned and will assist the tourist to find local attractions and services.

Perhaps the major new growth industry in San Juan County is high quality pottery. Utilizing the skills of young Navajo and Ute workers, an entire industry is developing in and around Blanding. Using mostly clays from the Mayfield area of Kentucky and locally blended paints, these young workers transform chunks of clay into incredibly brilliant, detailed and functional works of art. Most of the workers in the early portions of the process are hourly wage-earners, but the artists themselves are either working independently or under contract.

Other local artists prepare jewelry and paintings for sale to tourists and for shipment to wholesalers and retailers across the country. A large percentage of the artists in this developing industry are young adults with highly developed senses of proportion and color as well as steady nerve.

For the immediate future, the most likely economic growth will lie in tourism and in ceramics/pottery. The county made a strong pitch to be named the location for a new state prison. This would have meant a significant number of jobs. It would also have kept a significant number of local families in the immediate area. However the prison, if funded by the legislature, will go to another community closer to population centers.

Legal action has been threatened against San Juan County by one or more companies involved in oil field production. The claim is that since both the Navajo Nation, the Federal Government and the county are taxing the oil field production, there is multiple taxation, and it is illegal. The claim is that, like elsewhere across the nation, the county provides little or no service to the reservation.

The response of San Juan County is that the county provides more services than to county governments elsewhere in similar circumstances. San Juan County School District provides all the education for reservation children. San Juan County Highway and Road Department provides most road services for the reservation. Human services, community development, and county extension agent services are shared with the Navajo Nation. The county claims that the tax receipts from the oil fields on the reservation just about equal the cost of providing services to the reservation.

In Apache County, Arizona, just across the state line, the county provides a number of these services, but receives almost no tax revenues to offset the cost. In Apache County there is a movement to divide the county into reservation and non-reservation counties because of this problem.

Church

Two tiny United Methodist Churches, part of the Four Corners Ministry, serve the southern portion of the county. One, at Hatch Trading Post, has just been moved into position and will soon open its doors for worship. The other, at Oljato, has been in service for some time. United Methodist work in the county is almost exclusively among the Navajo.

The major religion in the area is Mormon. The claim in the area by the Church is that the county is 70% LDS or so. The actual percentage of participation in the Church is probably less than 30%. Other faiths, including Roman Catholic, Southern Baptist, Reformed, Assembly of God, and some Native American religions probably count another 20% participation. Probably half the county does not participate in any religious service during a particular calendar year.

The primary major impact of the LDS church on the county has come in its organized work of community development. In training leadership for its own needs the Church has performed a valuable service in developing community organization. The control exercised over the county by the LDS Church is an outgrowth of this intentional leadership development.

Another major impact of the LDS Church on the county has come from the Church's placement program. In this, young Native American children have been removed from their family home and raised in an Anglo home, typically in a distant community. Although the claim is that these persons are given a better education and access to the best cultural possibilities of Anglo society, there is not universal agreement on their value. The primary complaint within the community is that the children finally return home not knowing their ancestral language or culture, and not being accepted in the Anglo culture.

Most of the rest of the county churches sense themselves to be of a slightly lower economic and social class than the Mormons. Whether this is true is not documented, but the sense of it seems to create some difficulties for the congregations. This sense may simply be the result of living as a non-believer in a highly structured cultural system.

General

A large portion of the blame for the low per capita income of San Juan County in 1986 must be given to industries with a highly volatile potential and history. Oil, uranium, military work, and government agencies account for just about all the employment in the county. All these industries were in deep trouble in 1986 and continue in depression today.

The sole bright spots, as mentioned earlier, in the economy for the immediate future appear to be tourism and ceramics.

A more pervasive problem is the matter of limited retail sales in the county. The per capita rate of retail sales in San Juan County is less than half that of the state as a whole. As with the majority of the counties of this study, there is a Wal-Mart Store in the next county. In this instance, the Wal-Mart is in Cortez, Colorado, an hour's drive away.

The insistence on making most retail purchases in other counties has disastrous effects on local businesses and potential businesses. Instead of rolling over several times through a variety of businesses and activities within the county, the money that comes into the county is almost immediately taken out of the county and spent in Cortez, Moab, Shiprock, or Kayenta, Arizona. This deprives the county of jobs, profits, and economic stability. It also clearly allows the counties around San Juan County to benefit from the hard work of San Juan County residents more than do the San Juan County residents themselves.

San Juan County has great potential for retirement for middle income families. There are good medical and social services, a low cost of housing complete with some low income housing units, and a terrific climate. Recreation possibilities for easy outdoor access are almost limitless, especially if some low cost development occurs.

The county and the communities and the Navajo Nation are beginning to work feverishly toward stabilizing their economic climate. Their chief difficulty is and will continue to be some struggles between powerful groups in the communities and the persistent pattern of retail purchases in neighboring counties. A coherent effort at development, utilizing the services of the state, the county, the cities, and the Navajo Nation, will pay huge dividends for the future.

San Juan, Utah   Trend Information
Population and Households

	1970	1980	% Chg	1986	% Chg	1991	% Chg
	Census	Census	70-80	(Est.)	80-86	(Proj.)	86-91
Population	9606	12253	27.6	11637	-5.0	11104	-4.6
Households	2206	3018	36.8	2956	-2.1	2898	-2.0
Household Size	4.28*	4.04	-5.7	3.91	-3.1	3.81	-2.7
Group Quarters	65	65	0.0	65	0.0		
Income	1969	1979	% Chg	1986	% Chg	1991	% Chg
	Census	Census	69-79	(Est.)	79-86	(Proj.)	86-91
Agg. Income($mm)	16.4	45.3	176.9	52.2	15.1	54.5	4.4
Per Capita ($)	1705	3701	117.1	4484	21.2	4906	9.4
Average Hh ($)	7265	14718	102.6	17359	17.9	18481	6.5
Median Hh ($)	6220	13384	115.2	15562	16.3	16529	6.2
Household							
Income	1979		1986			1991	
Distribution	Count	%	Count	%	Count	%	
Less than $7,500	875	29.0	724	24.5	660	22.8	
$7,500 - $14,999	811	26.9	707	23.9	669	23.1	
$15,000 - $24,999	940	31.1	836	28.3	785	27.1	
$25,000 - $34,999	272	9.0	475	16.1	499	17.2	
$35,000 - $49,999	84	2.8	151	5.1	213	7.3	
$50,000 - $74,999	11	0.4	36	1.2	43	1.5	
$75,000 and over	25	0.8	27	0.9	29	1.0	

*1970 Household Size Is an Estimate Based on 1970 Census Data.
Data on Income Are Expressed in "Current" Dollars for Each Respective Year.
Hh=household   Agg=aggregate

Hispanic American

This segment might just as well be entitled "Rio Grande Culture Counties", for that is what they are. The prevailing language is Spanish and it is often difficult to find persons who can speak English.

But the populations of all these counties have at least large minorities of persons with direct ties with Spain. They also have large numbers of persons who have little or no Spanish ancestry, yet speak a tongue taken from the Spanish or from Catalan.

Many of the later arrivals in these counties are true Native Americans from southern Mexico or the Central American nations. Others are from the hilly country of northern Mexico. On one occasion, in Rio Grande City, I found it difficult to locate someone who spoke either Spanish or English. That little group was entirely from Guatemala (if I finally got the story straight).

The Rio Grande Culture is a culture of travel and transition, and has always been so. Wave after wave of population has swept up into the area from Central and South America, then been pushed farther up the river by later arrivals.

There is even some linguistic evidence that the Zuni people of New Mexico and Arizona are descended from Phoenicians who might have landed on the coast of Venezuela before the time of Christ. They then would have simply pushed their way north until they reached a permanent home. This happened to be in a rather hostile environment, but they have been allowed to reside there for a millennium or so.

It is known that the Navajo moved up the river along the same path many years later. We also know that the early Spaniards in the area were as far north as Colorado, Idaho, and Oregon before the middle of the 16th century, exploring for gold and slaves.

There is much conjecture about the Anasazi, the Ancient Ones, who lived in the area until around the end of the first millennium. We really do not know where they came from or what happened to them, but a likely chain of events seems possible.

It is probable that they came from someplace in Central or South America. They would have been pushed along by waves of immigrants coming behind them. At some point it seems that they might have made contact with immigrants or explorers coming from other areas.

These others might have been coming from the North, from Siberia through Alaska and Canada. Or, they might have been coming from the East, perhaps even from Scandinavia through New England and across. There is as yet no way to be certain.

But at some point one of two things almost certainly happened. Either they fell prey to a quickly spreading disease that wiped out whole communities within days, or an immense drought wiped out all of them within a year or two.

In either case, they simply ceased to exist. It is unlikely that they were all either killed or taken as slaves by marauders. Pockets of survivors would certainly have hung on. It seems more likely that a quick disease, perhaps some form of plague, wiped them out. The last remnants of the individual communities would have sought assistance from a neighboring pueblo, and thus unknowingly moved the plague along on its deadly course.

Another similar possibility is that the disease was not of humans, but of their crops. Some form of plant disease might have wiped them out in a year or two. The environment in the northern Rio Grande area is terribly harsh, viciously desperate. Killing the crops equates to killing the farmer.

This is the Rio Grande Culture. A huge community of people, always on the move. Even yet today masses of people move back and forth across the river for economic and family reasons. It is estimated that some 5 million persons cross the river at least once each year <u>for health care purposes alone</u>! Many others cross for their own varieties of reasons.

No nation, least of all the United States, has ever been able to stem the tide of incoming population. It is as though these waves of human desperation had a power beyond the power of any stationary government to stop them.

So this is the culture of the area. Moving, shifting, growing rapidly, and often in a confused state.

Conejos, Colorado
County Seat: Conejos
Geography

The Conejos (Rabbits) river, the largest tributary of the Rio Grande, has its headwaters in the remote South San Juan Wilderness Area. Blue, Green Red, and Glacier Lakes are a few of the gems in this unique playground. Platoro (silver-gold), once a vibrant mining town and now a growing resort community, adjoins America's largest lake over 9,900 feet elevation. Downstream the spectacular Conejos Canyon is noted as a top trout stream and vacation mecca. La Jara Reservoir provides elk hunting and fishing. Along the Alamosa River you will find the ghost towns of Jasper and Stunner around the red and yellow Lookout Mountain.

The Cumbres and Toltec Scenic Railway is one of the last narrow gauge railroads, and depots are located at Antonito and Chama, New Mexico. The line wanders along the Colorado-New Mexico border. Other historic attractions include the oldest church in Colorado, Pike's Stockade, Jack Dempsey's Birthplace, and old Spanish trails from Taos and Santa Fe.

Antonito, at the southern end of the San Luis Valley, is just six miles north of the New Mexico state line at an elevation of 7,888 feet. The San Luis valley is roughly an oval 100 miles long and 75 miles wide. Antonito is known as a "Perlite Capital of the World". This volcanic deposit is used in building materials, industrial filters, and cosmetics.

Platoro Reservoir is approximately 50 miles west of Antonito in the Conejos Canon at an elevation of 10,034 feet. The reservoir provides recreation and irrigation water for much of the valley.

The northern portion of Conejos County, around La Jara, is a rapidly developing agricultural area. Flat, and with good soil conditions, a developing potato industry is promising a good future.

United States Highway 285 leads on north to Alamosa, a thriving hub of the San Luis Valley culture and economy. With Adams State University, a variety of industries and commerce, and excellent human service care largely as the result of the work of various denominations, Alamosa is one of the most attractive residential communities in the county.

History

As part of the Rio Grande River drainage, the area now known as Conejos County has been home to a variety of peoples over the past several thousand years. The great San Luis Valley was home to a variety of civilizations that struggled with and against each other to find a place of good food, potential shelter, and reasonable climate.

Various populations found themselves either coming into the area by choice or being pushed them by population growth in other areas. Shortly before the Europeans came on the scene during the late 1600's, growing populations along the lower Rio Grande and in the southern plains pushed the people who were closer to the mountains into the high San Luis Valley. The Apaches and Utes were quite willing then to displace any previous residents and take command for themselves. Their struggles with each other were as much for pure rivalry as for survival.

The first Europeans, Spanish explorers and soldiers, came to the area only for excitement and for gold and silver. Mines in the area date from the middle of the 16th century.

The lower valley was actually settled beginning in 1854 with the arrival of major LaFayette Head and Selendonio Valdez. This first successful colony was at Servilleta, five miles east of the present town of Conejos.

Conejos became a town of considerable importance with a courthouse, a general store, the governor's palace and a flour mill. The Roman Catholic Church built Our Lady of Guadalupe Church, finishing it in 1866. It is known to be the oldest church in the state.

Because the first settlers were Spanish, and the area is part of the Rio Grande Basin, the community is a part of the Rio Grande culture. Spanish is commonly spoken in homes and businesses, although English is the general community language. Sixty-one percent of the population is Spanish origin. A very small percentage has roots in Mexico.

In Conejos County there is little note of ethnic struggles except in the northern end. There, more recent arrivals, the Mormons, have created some ethnic awareness. When considering their heritage, Hispanic persons in the county typically will trace directly back to Spain rather than note the bypass through Mexico. Most of the early residents could be noted as having lived in Mexico only because Texas, at that time, was a part of Mexico.

With the increased economic attractiveness of the United States, and greatly increasing populations of Mexico and Central America with their added turmoil and political strife, the county has seen a real increase in the immigrants both from south Texas and from Central America. The agriculture of the county no longer can use such hand labor, and no county manufacturing has ever needed such workers.

As with most of the counties of this study, Conejos County has a higher than average ratio of males to females, although there are still more women than men in the county. The social gauges are all low. The county has fewer than average marriages, divorces, crimes, and civil court cases. It is also understaffed for medical and social purposes.

In the United States, thirty percent of the families with female householders are below the poverty level. In Conejos County that figure is 41%, and 36% of all children are below the poverty level.

As with most of the counties in this study, few federal or state offices exist in the county except for the welfare office. Other offices that could be of major assistance to the residents have been regionalized, and their location moved to Alamosa, in this case. This move creates a further hardship for the citizens of Conejos County.

Antonito and Conejos are two of the oldest towns in the United States. At People's Drug Store in Antonito you can belly up to the hardwood counter and drink a milkshake made from hard ice cream and milk in an eight-beater milkshake maker. Have a little malt tossed in from the malt dispenser, and you have a little taste of the good life.

The communities have a bit of Old Spanish charm and graciousness in them. The people are warm and open to visitors, preferring to include strangers into their discussions and debates rather than shut them out. Visitor services are good and community agencies go out of their way to be helpful the traveling people, whether they be laborers, business travelers, or tourists.

Economy

Conejos County has been a thriving area at various times in its long life. Beginning with the gold and silver mined from the mountains in the western county, the economy has been on an up and down ride for over 300 years.

One factor that has created a large part of the current economic crunch is a demise of the fresh pea industry. At one time before the development of frozen food packaging and shipping methods Conejos county produced a major portion of the fresh English peas for eastern markets.

These peas were picked and packed by hand labor, loaded on iced railroad cars and trucks, and shipped off to Denver, Chicago, New York, and other areas clamoring for fresh vegetables. The traveling workers from Texas and Mexico came into the area by the thousands in the early summer to work the crops.

Eventually some of these workers stayed in the area, able to make a small transition from picking and packing in the fresh pea industry to the support operations such as planting, irrigating, cultivating, mechanical work, and management. Some of the workers found jobs in the secondary services industries, such as grocery stores, gas stations, and government.

With the coming of frozen food techniques, the hand work was no longer needed, and the great number of traveling workers just left, no longer to return. Stores began to close, housing slowed to a halt, and businesses went bankrupt.

For reasons of lack of capital for investment and lack of personal certainty that it could be done, the community did not make the shift from the fresh pea industry to the frozen pea industry. The entire economic structure was geared to the massive amounts of hand labor required in the fresh pea industry rather than to the few workers needed in the frozen pea industry.

With mechanization, and with the new technology, work that required a thousand workers in the old processes can be done by twenty-five in the new. This requires an enormous capital investment, however.

Shortly before the fresh pea market died, many of the farms came to be owned by absentee investors who were unwilling to risk large amounts of cash for the economic growth of the community. Many of the farms were converted to cattle operations which required far less capital for a good return (at that time), and almost no investment in a community processing plant. Necessary long term investment was just not made.

In recent years the county has been making a turn. Through a combination of factors, including an ambitious state program, a new sense of pride in the community is arising. The soil is good, the mountains are beautiful, the recreation in the area is second to none, and the potential for a variety of economic development work is outstanding. The community is pressing ahead on a drive for economic development, and some progress is being made, particularly in agriculture and in tourism.

Vacation and retirement homes are becoming popular in the area. There is some potential for a water impoundment project which would create a great area for water skiing, fishing, and cruising. The county is becoming aware of its history as the Crown of the Rio Grande, and additional moves are being made to advertise the goodness of the area.

Church

While Conejos County does not have a United Methodist Church, much mission work is carried on through the congregation at Alamosa. Both the larger church and the congregation at Alamosa have committed good funds and effort to the development of Christian Community Services, Inc. That group actually is the primary human services agency for Conejos county as well as several others. The General Board of Global Ministries has been a large part of this work.

Christian Community Services provides a great deal of ministry in the whole area, including such packages as counseling, gleaning, housing assistance, clothing, food supplies, and many other ministries. While it serves six counties, it appears that much of its work is focused on Conejos and Costilla Counties, the two poorest in the area. In fact, most people in that area will state that Costilla County is poorer than is Conejos County.

The oldest church in the state is in Conejos, the county seat. This Catholic church has been active since 1830 or so. However, as so many Roman Catholic churches today, a real shortage of priests is limiting its work. While the congregation gets a strong share of displeasure from the community for its lack of participation in the community life as a whole, it seems that much of this might be traced to this lack of personnel. Sixty percent of the population of the county is Roman Catholic. The building apparently will seat about 250 for worship.

Other congregations in the area include a strong Mormon group in the northern portion of the county, around La Jara. This group is rather active, including such things as Scouts, welfare practices, recreation, and economic development in the area. Their building will seat around 250.

Other churches in the area include small Churches of Christ, Baptist Churches, and Assemblies of God. Church affiliation is said to be 62.3% Roman Catholic, 31.7% L.D.S., 3% Assembly of God, and less than 1% for the Church of Christ and Mennonites.

The future of Conejos appears to hold promise in tourism, retirement housing, some mineral deposits and perhaps some revitalization of a dead agriculture. The climate is very good for all these activities. The county only awaits the structures to make them realities.

Conejos, Colorado   Trend Information

Population and Households

	1970	1980	% Chg	1986	% Chg	1991	% Chg
	Census	Census	70-80	(Est.)	80-86	(Proj.)	86-91
Population	7846	7794	-0.7	8161	4.7	8455	3.6
Households	1980	2356	19.0	2553	8.4	2725	6.7
Household Size	3.93*	3.31	-15.9	3.20	-3.4	3.10	-2.9
Group Quarters	0	0	0.0	0	0.0		
Income	1969	1979	% Chg	1986	% Chg	1991	% Chg
	Census	Census	69-79	(Est.)	79-86	(Proj.)	86-91
Agg. Income($mm)	10.3	25.6	147.6	35.9	40.1	42.7	18.9
Per Capita ($)	1318	3285	149.2	4396	33.8	5045	14.8
Average Hh ($)	5204	10755	106.7	13910	29.3	15499	11.4
Median Hh ($)	4927	9071	84.1	11711	29.1	12925	10.4
Household	Income	Distribution					
	1979		1986		1991		
	Count	%	Count	%	Count	%	
Less than $ 7,500	1012	43.0	838	32.8	794	29.1	
$ 7,500 - $14,999	801	34.0	781	30.6	786	28.8	
$15,000 - $24,999	396	16.8	583	22.8	648	23.8	
$25,000 - $34,999	111	4.7	229	9.0	306	11.2	
$35,000 - $49,999	30	1.3	96	3.8	142	5.2	
$50,000 - $74,999	6	0.3	22	0.9	40	1.5	
$75,000 and over	0	0.0	4	0.2	9	0.3	

*1970 Household Size Is an Estimate Based on 1970 Census Data.
Data on Income Are Expressed in "Current" Dollars for Each Respective Year.
Hh=household   Agg=aggregate

Mora, New Mexico
County Seat: Mora
Geography

Mora County is located some 30 miles north of Las Vegas, New Mexico, on the eastern slope of the Rockies. The eastern portion of the county is crossed by Interstate 25. New Mexico Highways 121, 3, 38, 94, 21, and 161 run through the county. The eastern portion is a high valley area, a broad a flat area suitable basically for livestock only.

The western portion of the county covers the start of the rougher foothills that make up the wider area of the Rockies. The village of Mora itself with its surrounding small villages and settlements, sets in a picturesque valley. The primary route between Las Vegas and Taos runs through Mora.

In spite of the mountainous terrain and occasional blizzards which dump immense amounts of snows in the area the winters in Mora County are not really severe. Snows generally melt in a few days, and travel becomes relatively easy again.

The valley floor is small river plain with only a few areas of western Mora County suitable for tilling. The slopes provide good rootage for pines and other conifers. The timber is not thick because limited rainfall in the area inhibits the growth, but it is commercially valuable.

The total land area of the county is 1,930 square miles. Much of the land is in the Carson and the Santa Fe National Forests, Fort Union National Monument, three state parks, and many historical areas.

The thirty mile distance to Las Vegas makes it practical to do much shopping there, as well as commute for work and for education. New Mexico Highlands at Las Vegas provides a well rounded education.

History

Mora County has never been a prosperous area. Like most of the counties in northern New Mexico, Mora County has been the site of a lot of pushing and shoving between native cultures and peoples for several thousand years.

The Spanish explorers and soldiers came into the county in the 1600's, pushing along the Navaho who had pushed the Apache who had pushed someone else. Ninety percent of the population is listed as Spanish origin. The long-time Spanish origin residents of Mora County now are descendants of the old line Spanish rather than of Mexican heritage. Few of Mexican heritage settled in the area until recent years when some Texas Mexican families entered. However, these have really not had a major impact on the community because of the small numbers and the wide areas for settlement.

The closest thing Mora County has ever had to a thriving economy has been just the development of a lot of service and retail industry that has operated on very little amounts of incoming cash. The highway through Mora is lined with many small "mom and pop" stores that have operated from homes, garages, small buildings, or even from vehicles until the operators became to old and tired to carry on. Then those business just close, for there are no buyers of the businesses.

The population of Mora County is not in any sense a transient community, and the median age in the county at twenty nine is considerably higher than the state median. People tend to come and stay, not making much money but living comfortably with the climate and the community.

Birth, death, marriage, and divorce rates in Mora County tend to approximate the national averages. This is a variance from the rest of the counties in this study. Reported serious crimes are about 8% of the national average.

Poverty for female householders is a serious matter. Nearly 70% of the households headed by a female are below the poverty level. This reflects the sad truth that there are just very few jobs in the area and even fewer that are traditionally known as women's jobs. In addition, in most two-parent families, both parents are working if they can find employment.

Suicide or suicidal thinking within the community seems to be a real problem, although many of the suicide deaths appear to be labeled as accidents, both of teenagers and the elderly.

Mora County history is really quite simple. With an economy based on small business rather than on sudden immense wealth, not many groups or persons have tried to take over the area. As mentioned earlier, the fishing and hunting and small gardening in the area has made for a relatively easy life style, but these are not the attractions for a power hungry horde of raiders.

Many of the Native American peoples now on reservations throughout the Southwest were pushed at times through this area by their conquerors, whether human or natural. Hunger, drought, and disease often brought the ancient peoples into the area searching for survival.

But none have stayed as long as the Spanish, who have set up their good little civilization, and have called it home now for several centuries. The reality is that living in the area is felt to be `so good' that people who are prone to settlements rather than wandering tribes really don't want to leave. In spite of the rather precarious economic realities of the community, no one I talked to in the community was seriously looking for a way to leave.

There is some possibility of a power play now going through the community that tends to add a little excitement, although it might be somewhat harmful to the economy. There are rumors that various persons of prestige in the community are attempting to control the government development programs that seem to be springing up across the county. As anywhere else, those involved in development are recognized as being first interested in lining their own pockets. In a small county, this is more likely seen as "taking it out of my pocket and putting it in yours". Violent acts aimed at these developers have been a part of the past.

With no organized cities in the county, all the politics of the area are centered in the county government, and the Commissioners are really the recognized leaders of the area. These people tend to have a little more power than those in areas with incorporated cities.

There is a possibility that this tendency can be used to good advantage if the county can focus in on the type of economic development it chooses to follow. Several small business operators in the county spoke of the need to come together to make some decisions about economic development.

Economy

The economic framework of Mora County has never been very strong, and at this point there seems to be little hope of good development in the near future. However, the county does offer some hope for the long run.

First, mountain recreation such as skiing, hiking, snowmobiling, fishing, and hunting are on the rise. The development of the Angel Fire Resort near Taos has given several persons from Mora County permanent or seasonal employment.

Second, small business is coming back. The motel in Mora is as comfortable as any small motel anywhere. Several restaurants and small grocery stores have come into being in the last few years, some in the face of violence. These operations, while not providing employment and income to thousands, do provide a living to dozens, and that helps.

Third, the Mora Valley and the surrounding hillsides are some of the best land available for conifers, especially for such specialty products as Christmas trees. The New Mexico University system has developed a tree known as the Afghan Pine which thrives in the valley, creating a beautiful six-foot tree in two years at its normal rate of growth.

The development of a Christmas tree market and industry would be a major factor in the area for several reasons. Christmas trees can be grown in small lots, and the skill needed in growing, shaping, harvesting, and marketing the trees can be readily taught. This might pave the way for single parents to become more self-supporting without the requirement of leaving the children day after day with a babysitter. Christmas trees are labor intensive, allowing the producer to work without huge investments of capital for processing. Wholesalers of the trees take them from a central gathering point or from a field, depending on the arrangement, making it possible to harvest without locking up an enormous amount of time at any one point in the process.

Greg Fancher at the Agricultural Experiment Station sees Christmas trees as a good alternative crop for small farmers in the area. There is an expectation that major tree farming operations will move into the community before the small operators get their processes together, but most hope the small operators will be able to survive.

Perhaps the greatest asset of the Experiment Station is the systemic operational and personal culture that surrounds it. By working in the most intentional way to display good working practices to the community, the Station attempts to be a good model for the community. The obvious pride in the operation on the part of the workers seems to rub off on the rest of the community. People across the valley spoke with admiration, not just of the horticultural advances of the station, but of the "good crew", and the "fine people" at the experiment station. The community is convinced the workers at the station really care. However, they find it difficult to believe that the state really has any part of an intentionality of caring.

One of the major heartaches and headaches of the county is that the county itself is bankrupt. Broke. The state has taken control of all fiscal matters of the county in order to allow the bills to be paid and work to be carried on. This is seen as a source of embarrassment in the county by both the county employees and the taxpayers. It hurts.

Almost every person interviewed in the county began the conversation with the notification that the county was broke. Few, however, understood what would have to happen to regain solvency.

The county operates without a regular budget, requiring that only necessary expenditures be made to keep things moving along. This negates any intentional economic development which requires even a few dollars capitalization.

The impact of this whole system appears to be that persons cannot make long-term contracts or other commitments. They just do not trust the future. This may be the reason that most of the counties in this study have a lower than average marriage rate. Even applications for welfare assistance must be made in another county.

The educational system in the county is struggling, in part because of low pay for teachers and other staff, and in part because many do not see that education is any way to get into a better life. Because most want to stay in Mora County, and educational level really doesn't seem to make much difference in whether one is making it financially in Mora County, why study?

It is rumored that the county stopped the development of a brewery and a fish hatchery in the area because of a power struggle. Whether this is true is perhaps debatable, but the accusation of willful defeat of economic development, especially in the case of the fish hatchery, is a serious one. It is part of the violence of the county's image of itself.

So what are the benefits of living and working in Mora County? First, this would be a good place to retire on a modest income. There are many opportunities to semi-retire and make a small living at a garage business or a one person operation. Good houses rent for $150-$250 per month. The climate is great, and the scenery is fantastic. In an hour or so one can be in a totally different environment, city or desert.

Second, small business operators here who can develop systems to make profits off the natural gifts of the land and the people will be honored by the community, especially if you enable someone else to make a few dollars also.

Third, as Alfredo Roybal at the Chevron Station said, "There is lots of money here because there is no place to spend it."

Many persons who grew up in the community and left to go to college or to establish homes elsewhere are now returning to the community for permanent residence or for vacation homes. Like it or not, growth is an industry in Mora County.

<u>Church</u>

There is no evidence of any United Methodist work in Mora County. The United Presbyterian Church has been active there, although there is not a resident pastor in the county. The little congregation seems to be the only congregation in the county with any reputation for community service in any way. In addition, some of the members there are on various national and international Presbyterian program and study groups. Some have made trips into Central America and other areas with fact-finding groups. The congregation is served by a pastor who lives in a neighboring county.

There is a Roman Catholic Church, an Assembly of God, a Baptist Church, three Churches of Christ, and some smaller churches. Ninety-five percent of the population is considered by some to be Roman Catholic. It appears that active community support by the Church does not exist.

Mora, New Mexico   Trend Information
Population and Households

	1970	1980	% Chg	1986	% Chg	1991	% Chg
	Census	Census	70-80	(Est.)	80-86	(Proj.)	86-91
Population	4673	4205	-10.0	5111	21.5	5857	14.6
Households	1280	1390	8.6	1743	25.4	2053	17.8
Household Size	3.64*	3.03	-16.9	2.93	-3.1	2.85	-2.7
Group Quarters	0	0	0.0	0	0.0		
Income	1969	1979	% Chg	1986	% Chg	1991	% Chg
	Census	Census	69-79	(Est.)	79-86	(Proj.)	86-91
Agg. Income($mm)	4.9	14.3	192.3	24.2	69.1	32.5	34.4
Per Capita ($)	1048	3404	224.8	4737	39.2	5554	17.2
Average Hh ($)	3821	10066	163.4	13555	34.7	15462	14.1
Median Hh ($)	4252	7663	80.2	11021	43.8	12484	13.3
Household	Income	Distribution					
	1979			1986		1991	
	Count	%		Count	%	Count	%
Less than $ 7,500	696	50.1		641	36.8	655	31.9
$ 7,500 - $14,999	365	26.3		491	28.2	559	27.2
$15,000 - $24,999	275	19.8		349	20.0	427	20.8
$25,000 - $34,999	42	3.0		206	11.8	260	12.7
$35,000 - $49,999	6	0.4		45	2.6	132	6.4
$50,000 - $74,999	0	0.0		4	0.2	12	0.6
$75,000 and over	6	0.4		7	0.4	8	0.4

*1970 Household Size Is an Estimate Based on 1970 Census Data.
Data on Income Are Expressed in "Current" Dollars for Each Respective Year.
Hh=household   Agg=aggregate

Maverick, Texas
County Seat: Eagle Pass

Geography

Maverick County is a bedroom and shopping suburb of the much larger Piedras Negras across the Rio Grande River. With about the same overall gross economy until these last few years, and about ten times the number of persons, Piedras Negras has been a study in poverty. Eagle Pass has been the recipient of considerable traffic from across the river.

The county, with a total land area of 1287 square miles and a population of about 25,000 person, is sparsely populated except in Eagle Pass itself. There are several much smaller communities scattered along the Rio Grande River. These communities are basically farming communities. The land rises fairly rapidly from the river, but then begins a gently rolling terrain. This gentle rolling terrain covers most of the county.

The river itself, apart from symbolizing the border between the United States and Mexico, commands the livelihood of a large number of persons from Colorado to the Gulf of Mexico. The river valley, though small by long river standards, has functioned over several thousand years as the central pipeline of an extensive culture and civilization.

The river valley has also provided water, both surface, ground, and in the attraction of precipitation, for a rather healthy agriculture. The easy availability of workers coming north out of Mexico and Central America has always kept wages quite low, although the cost of living has remained low until recent years. Although roads and railroads have existed between that area and other Texas cities for most of recorded history, it has only been since the coming of major industries to the area that transportation systems have begun to be on a par with those in other parts of the county.

The prevailing soils are sandy loam to rich alluvial. Scattered mesquite, some live oak, cat's claw, huajilla, cenizo, and prickly pear are the predominate flora. Animal life includes white tail deer, skunks, coyotes, javelinas, armadillos, jack rabbits, wild turkey, dove, quail, and rattlesnakes. Some natural gas and oil are produced, and deposits of cannel coal and clay are available. Coal mining is still done across the river.

History

The county was created in 1856, organized in 1871, and named for Samuel Augustus Maverick. After the Texas Revolution, the Mexican government forbade a direct trade with the Texans. However, Mexican villages near the Rio Grande continued to trade clandestinely with San Antonio by using a trail which ran to the north of the old roads. This crossing of the river took its name from the flights of eagles that made their aeries in the ancient pecan trees along the Escondido Creek.

Early settlers of Eagle Pass were discharged soldiers who along with stranded emigrants on the California trail stayed to ranch or trade across the border. A stage line reached Eagle Pass as early as 1851. All through the decade preceding the Civil War, Eagle Pass was a haven for out-laws, slave hunters, and assorted types of border bad men. By 1872 the Southern Pacific Railroad had arrived, and the telegraph came in 1875.

Through the late 1870's an outlaw named King Fisher controlled the town, the Texas Rangers restored order under the leadership of L.H. McNally and Lee Hall. A private school for girls opened in 1883 at about the same time the first permanent bank was opening in the county.

In April, 1932, a large gravity irrigation project from a Rio Grande intake forty miles up the river went into operation under the Maverick County Water Control and Improvement District. This brought water into the Quemado district for the first time. At this time the canal system consists of over 300 miles of canals, providing water for the three-crop-per-year agriculture.

Population

The population of Maverick County has grown steadily up until 1970. Since that time the population of the county has doubled, and will probably double again before the end of the century. At the same time household size has shrunk by 10%, and will probably continue to shrink. Reasons for this include the very drastic changes in the traveling worker patterns which will be discussed under economy.

Ninety percent of the population of Maverick County is Hispanic, although 52% of the population was born in Texas. Part of the reason for this relatively low percentage of those born in Texas is that the best medical care in this region is that given at low cost at the government hospital in Piedras Negras. Eagle Pass is a middle to upper class suburb to Piedras Negras, and many of the residents take advantage of the best parts of the social services delivery systems on both sides of the river.

The hospital at Piedras Negras is widely known for its surgical experience, including heart surgery and neurological techniques. It has the reputation of attracting some of the best physicians in Mexico because of its proximity to the United States.

Although the overall birth rate in Maverick County is nearly double the national average, the ratio of births to mothers under the age of 20 is about the national level. There are about half again the ratio of marriages as the national averages and about half the divorce ratio. Significantly, the county reports about eighty percent of the national ratio for general serious crimes and for violent crimes in particular.

Economy

The economy of Maverick County has gone up and down with the state of international politics and economics. Up until the end of World War II the major economy supporting Eagle Pass was agriculture and commerce with Mexico. Since then a number of industries have located in the Eagle Pass-Maverick County area. These include the Eagle Pass Manufacturing Company and the Williamson-Dickie Manufacturing Company, both makers of work clothing. There is also the Reynolds Mining Corporation fluorspar plant and the Tejas Barite plant; Alta Verde Industries and Maverick Beef Producers, both cattle feeding operations, and the Big River Catfish Farm, a producer of frozen fish. Other industries include a broom factory, two cotton gins, a vegetable packing and shipping plant, a meat packing plant, the Don Career Manufacturing Company, and the Central Power and Light Company hydro-electric plan on the Rio Grande.

The county now has approximately 300 producing oil wells. Both the city and the county governments have begun a variety of projects aimed at improving its business economy, including a new and enlarged airport near Eagle Pass.

Maverick County expects a good economic position in industry, tourism, recreation, and retirement service. Good climate, an aggressive development program, a very large actual available labor force, and a modern city would seem to bode well for the future.

Maquilladoras

Under the twin plant concept, American firms may export American made components to Mexico for assembly and then import the assembled product back into the U.S.A. at preferential tariff rates.

This program is called the "Twin Plant Program" because many manufacturers have found that having an assembly operation in Mexico, coupled with a nearby twin production or distribution operation in Texas, is a very efficient facilities configuration. This location pattern takes advantage of the best of the two nation's economic resources.

A Texas location provides access to the nation's fastest growing markets, skilled labor pools, excellent transportation and utility networks, and all the other benefits of the American Sunbelt economy. Because much of Texas, particularly along the Rio Grande River, speaks more Spanish than English, few cultural barriers to such cross industrialization processes exist.

The principal advantage to companies operating twin plant facilities in Mexico is an abundant supply of low skill, low cost, highly productive labor. Millions of Mexicans fight for the opportunity to work in such plants, even if it means living in squalor. Piedras Negras has tens of thousands of persons living in cardboard hovels and fighting for a chance to make less for a month of hard labor than many U.S. workers make in a day.

In spite of the success of the maquilladoras, other events are taking shape that will impact the economic future of the area. American labor unions are becoming aware of and openly critical of the Maquilladoras. Legislation is being considered in congress as well as in the various legislatures which would seriously handicap the twin plant operations.

Perhaps a more serious problem are the reported human rights violations in the Mexican plants themselves. Because a large majority of the employees in the Mexican plants are women, and there is simply no other major work for women in the areas, stories frequently arise about sexual harassment in the work place. Other persons report over work, threats of firings for want of kickback, and other abuses. Some of these are periodically documented by regional newspapers and other media.

In recent years Maverick County has attempted to show that it can have a life and economy apart from that of Piedras Negras. The attempts to attract industry and other economic financial strength have helped, and apparently have made some good increases in self-confidence and personal self esteem within the community. The truth, though, is that as a suburb of Piedras Negras, Eagle Pass would not be able to function in any good economic way without the rather strange economy of Piedras Negras across the river.

Church

In Maverick County there are three United Methodist Churches, all seemingly doing fairly well. There are Anglo congregations at Eagle Pass and Quemado, part of the Southwest Texas Annual Conference, Kerrville District. The Hispanic congregation at Eagle Pass is part of the Rio Grande Missionary Conference.

The Anglo congregation at Eagle Pass is a very traditional downtown church, with a location directly across from the new county courthouse. It has good grounds, and performs a variety of community services. However, such matters as education and evangelism are not assertively pursued. The pastor, Bill Sandefer, also serves the congregation at Quemado. He also appears to be personally responsible for most of the community service work of the congregation.

The Anglo congregation at Eagle Pass handles the funds for the United Way / Salvation Army relief program. There is some suspicion that Hispanic persons are systematically referred to the Hispanic congregation for assistance, but I question that.

The congregation seems to be frustrated by the limited numbers of English-speaking persons in the community. However, it does appear that the congregation is ready to take significant steps toward growth. The membership stands at about 60, and the entire church budget is just over $10,000 per year.

Attendance seems to average about 30 persons, with only two or three in attendance at church school. There is an active United Methodist Women organization, involved in a variety of service and study projects.

At the Hispanic congregation, the congregation is preparing to make some additions to their building. They need a little space. They are woefully short of educational and fellowship space. This is the more evangelistic of the congregations.

Benjamin Villanueva has this congregation in an upwardly mobile transition period, although the congregation is not wealthy. Many of their people "travel" in the summer, either for work or for vacation.

One major issue at La Trinidad is the request that Vacation Church School material be in English rather than in Spanish. English is understood to be the language of upward economic mobility, and the insistence that the children be taught to read and write Spanish rather than English is understood to be a racist ploy.

The congregation at Quemado is small, but apparently a strong and contributive part of the community. Many of the decisions are made on the church steps, and the pastor is informed later, which is typical for churches of this size. Neither the church at Eagle Pass or the church at Quemado seems to have a good sense of their potential.

The Quemado congregation, in fact, may be the base from which a very strong ministry might be established. The personal descriptions of the situation describe a strong, educated, successful, and committed congregation, limited only by their sense of being quite small.

At La Trinidad (the Hispanic Church in Eagle Pass) it is important to note that the Villanuevas are very comfortable on both sides of the Rio Grande. Her parents are store owners in Piedras Negras, and they move back and forth with good ease, including contacts with the Methodist Church in Piedras Negras. Many of their members have this same lifestyle.

Eagle Pass is only recently learning that it can have a life of its own apart from ties with Piedras Negras. Even the churches seem burdened with the sense of being suburban to a great impoverished people on the other side of the river. In reality, however, I would suspect that the two Eagle Pass congregations could have pretty good work on their own without paying much attention to Piedras Negras. That would not help the folks in Piedras Negras, of course, but it is a heavy load for the two congregations in one of the poorest counties in the US to attempt to work with the Church in an even poorer neighboring city.

MAVERICK, TEXAS   TREND INFORMATION
POPULATION AND HOUSEHOLDS

	1970	1980	% CHG	1986	% CHG	1991	% CHG
	CENSUS	CENSUS	70-80	(EST.)	80-86	(PROJ.)	86-91
POPULATION	18093	31398	73.5	36902	17.5	41417	12.2
HOUSEHOLDS	4097	7583	85.1	9224	21.6	10666	15.6
HOUSEHOLD SIZE	4.39*	4.05	-7.8	3.92	-3.0	3.82	-2.7
GROUP QUARTERS	721	721	0.0	721	0.0		
INCOME	1969	1979	% CHG	1986	% CHG	1991	% CHG
	CENSUS	CENSUS	69-79	(EST.)	79-86	(PROJ.)	86-91
AGG. INCOME($MM)	23.2	97.3	319.6	148.0	52.1	187.7	26.8
PER CAPITA ($)	1282	3100	141.8	4011	29.4	4532	13.0
AVERAGE HH ($)	5647	12454	120.5	15648	25.6	17180	9.8
MEDIAN HH ($)	5169	10026	94.0	12522	24.9	13624	8.8
HOUSEHOLD							
INCOME	1979		1986		1991		
DISTRIBUTION	COUNT	%	COUNT	%	COUNT	%	
LESS THAN $ 7,500	3002	39.6	2875	31.2	2991	28.0	
$ 7,500 - $14,999	2329	30.7	2594	28.1	2868	26.9	
$15,000 - $24,999	1559	20.6	2122	23.0	2476	23.2	
$25,000 - $34,999	450	5.9	1028	11.1	1352	12.7	
$35,000 - $49,999	126	1.7	393	4.3	663	6.2	
$50,000 - $74,999	77	1.0	115	1.2	182	1.7	
$75,000 AND OVER	40	0.5	97	1.1	134	1.3	

Starr, Texas
County Seat: Rio Grande City

Starr County is a historic county about one hundred miles inland from Brownsville along the Rio Grande River. Thousands of years of population and culture waves coursing through and around the area have left communities ill prepared to work together for economic development.

Geography

Starr County covers 1,226 square miles of southernmost Texas. Spreading north from the Rio Grande River, Starr County changes from flat flood plain along the river to rolling hills and eroded cliffs through the primary residential sections to open lightly rolling plains in the north. The relation of the county to the Rio Grande River is the most significant geographical and geological notation. It is also a primary factor in the madcap economy of the area.

The county has two incorporated cities, although other communities are considering incorporation. Rio Grande City, where the county courthouse is located, is not incorporated. This is a factor in economic weakness in the area as coordinated planning and growth is not taking place. The growth that is occurring is generally uncontrolled. The growth takes place by individual initiative rather than by community effort.

Along both the east and west boundaries of the county are found the oil fields. These wells have not been the most productive in Texas but they have produced good income, mostly for out of county investors.

The north central portion of the county is largely uninhabited with very limited access by road. The El Negro Ranch covers a significant portion of this area.

US Highway 83 is the primary route through the county from east to west. This highway parallels the Rio Grande River, and is also the main street of most of the settlements in the county. La Grulla is the only community of any size in the south that is not directly located on Highway 83.

Starr County receives an average of 17 inches of rain per year. May is the month of heaviest precipitation. It rarely rains in August.

History

Starr County has a history as open and exciting as any county in the nation, but because of the nature of that history it will never be completely told. Migratory and commercial traffic back and forth across the Mexican-American border has never really been heavy at the three crossings in Starr County. The bulk of regular traffic in the area has crossed either down river or upriver from Starr County. This lack of the kind of international traffic that would bring wealth has not helped Starr County.

Not even traveling farm workers have come through Starr County. Starr County has some very productive farms along the river, but these operate year round with local labor.

Historically, it is said that most of the people who just wanted to get back and forth across the river in the ordinary course of their lives have been able to do so comfortably at Starr County. On several occasions it appears that these `ordinary people' have been able to find other reasons for crossing, and Starr County bridges have provided easy access. Early guerrilla actions, banditry, and today's narcotics traffic appear to be primary beneficiaries of this relative ease of access between the nations.

From the earliest years of recorded history it has not been possible to separate culturally or economically the north bank and south bank people of the Rio Grande River Valley. For instance, Starr County population is about 96% Hispanic, with most of the families able to trace their roots in the area back several hundred years. Most of these families have moved back and forth between the nations relatively freely regardless of international politics and economics.

Through the nineteenth century steamboats plied the Rio Grande River bringing economic life to the valley as far inland as the boats could travel. At various times rafts brought goods down the river for sale to the buyers on the trading steamers. While this was never as successful as was the trade on the Mississippi, it did contribute heavily to the early decision to place the limits of Texas at the river rather than a more northerly location.

Starr County has apparently not until recent years been a very peaceful community. With a culture used to dealing with kings and dictators and emperors, a few families seem to have been able to dictate the politics and economics and church life of Starr County. Even today the fact that Rio Grande City is not incorporated appears to reflect decisions by families in other parts of the county to limit the growth and influence of Rio Grande City. The relationship between them is something akin to the relationship between Washington, D.C., and New York City.

This stormy relationship has had its problems. Rumors abound of various business activities being driven from the county by one or more of the strong leadership groups. Whether these rumors are true is a matter of conjecture in most instances. Several persons in authority positions did relate one incident of a major retail chain being barred from the county.

It has not been too long since the county had only one political party. It was charged that this party was under the control of one family in the county. Whether the charge was true is not documented, but the outgrowth of the charge was the development of three more political parties in the county. In the culture of the Rio Grande River, family and community are supremely important. This fierce loyalty seems to have been translated into fiercely committed political action.

This growing portion of the community life, if harnessed, may be the agency for transforming a stagnating economy into a real growth pattern. If the county can learn to back its own businesses with the same loyalty and community pride, and organize the communities to give wings to this loyalty and pride, the county may have a great future. Although current projections typically reflect a lesser growth rate, I would not be surprised to see a city of some five million persons in the Roma to Brownsville corridor early in the twenty first century.

When Spanish settlers first came to the valley they were allotted 'porciones.' These strips of land were one mile wide and eleven miles long, running up from the river. The apparent reason for the shape was to give the most feasible configuration for cattle operations to the most possible people. Cattle can readily make an eleven mile trek for water.

But as two and a half centuries have gone by, all the original owners are dead, and they or their successors have either sold or given away parts of the land. Some of the porciones were simply inherited by larger and larger numbers of people. The family is very important.

Most of these title changes were done without benefit of survey, leaving the ownership in utter confusion. In some cases the courts have officially divided the land by survey and decision. Someone has taken the time (and the money) to have the task done properly, relying on the laws and whatever Solomon like wisdom the court has to allot the lands appropriately.

Thirteen of these porciones in the county are as yet undivided, meaning that clear title can not be obtained on over fifty five thousand acres of the best farmland and the most developable areas of the county. This situation produces sometimes laughable and generally tragic results.

Without clear title one cannot get a mortgage lien for a loan. Many persons in the county have legal documents attesting to ownership of land that cannot be located. Many persons are paying taxes on land that they cannot find, much less use. If they quit paying the taxes, they lose any claim to a future disposition. On much of the land, any person who has such a claim cannot be evicted from any part of the porcione.

Attempts to resolved these matters have resulted in family and community struggles. The long-term effect has been the denial of a number of economic development activities that would have helped the county.

Starr County, and particularly Old Rio Grande City, would make an ideal setting for Rio Grande Culture movies and tourist activities. The architecture and community layout is truly a combination of Mexican and U.S. thought. Some work is being done to restore Old Rio Grande City.

The La Borde House, a fine hotel dating from 1899, recalls the glory days of the area. It is one of the most picturesque and comfortable resting places in the nation.

Francoise La Borde came to the area in the 1880's to complete his fortune. He commissioned an architect from Paris to design an appropriate home for him in this bustling community. Lumber for the original construction was brought upriver on a stern-wheeler, and mesquite fired yellow clay brick was imported from Camargo, Mexico. The result is a combination Creole, Texas Border and Victorian masterpiece of graciousness and charm.

Today the county is slowly redeveloping commercial activity, although with little planning and organization. It is charged by officials and acknowledged on the streets that drug running is the most lucrative activity in the county.

Population

With a population of nearly 30,000, Starr County is a strong candidate for commercial development. Its 22 persons per square mile keep it in the low density range for both the state and the nation.

About 97% of the population is Hispanic. It is said locally that nearly all the non-Hispanic persons in the county are professionals who have come to the county with jobs in government or services such as motel chains and supermarket chains. There are several Anglo farm operators. Ethnic origin does not seem to be a major issue here.

Starr County is a young county. The median age is 22 and 10 % of the population is under 5 years of age compared with 30 and 7.2% for the nation as a whole. Only 9% of the county population is over 65, compared with 12 % for the nation as a whole.

The birth rate in the county is nearly double the national average, but births to women under the age of 20 are at about the national average. The marriage rate is high, and for the calendar year 1983 no divorces were reported completed in the county.

The serious crime rate is about 20% of the state and national average, although a larger number of crimes appear to go un-solved each year. Drug traffic is apparently a large factor.

In 1983 about 15 % of the homes in the county lacked complete plumbing facilities, and 29% of the homes had more than 1.1 persons per room. Eighty percent, a very large number, of the homes in the county were owner occupied.

Illiteracy is high. Almost every source interviewed in the county spoke of the need for expanded literacy programs. Some persons blame the lack of bilingual education. Other persons blame the existence of bilingual education. Only 26% of the population has complete high school. Some estimate that at least 50% of the population can neither read nor write anything beyond their own name in any language.

Unemployment in the county generally is listed between 30% and 40%, year in and year out. Actual unemployment, including persons who have just given up looking for work, is probably at least double that figure. About half of all families are listed as living below the poverty level.

The population of Starr County is not a transient population. The people, when they move, tend to move within the state. In fact, 72% of the population of the county was born in Texas, compared with a state average of 67.8 and a national average of 63.9.

Economy

The current economic framework of Starr County is built on a culture that provides a drastic break between the upper and lower economic classes and very little middle class. One impact of this is that those trapped in the lower economic groups tend to believe that there is no way to escape poverty legally.

The really attractive industry in economic terms is drug traffic. This county, which is officially listed as the fourth poorest county in the United States, has at least several dozen homes that would rank with the best mansions of Long Island or Dallas. Some of these are owned by legitimate business operators or retired professionals.

This traffic is not too different from the way some of the other portions of the county economy operate. I have already mentioned the trouble with undivided porciones. The list of uncollected taxes is extensive. Officials in the county would not comment on this. One source said "Of course the county won't collect the taxes. How would they be reelected?" These issues have a strong effect on the county.

Agriculture along the Rio Grande River has been a staple of the county economy for centuries. Two factors have made this industry much less attractive at the moment. First, high mechanization of farming as a whole has released millions of people across the land from their sole employment.

While this part of the package has been helpful to the farm operator, there are problems. The immense cost of farm machinery and high interest rates create a different business climate. Additionally, more complex machinery calls for a new class of mechanic, and persons in this field are demanding higher and higher wages for their services. Added fuel costs and lower tax breaks add to the woes. To top it off, the self-image of the farm family as a cohesive unit, working and laughing and praying together, is taking a beating as developers break up more and more good old communities for residences of commuters.

The second factor is the weakness of community commitment and pride. Farming rarely is successful outside cooperative ventures of some sort. The best marketing procedures are those which bring a number of operators together in a cooperative effort. The best purchasing of supplies and hiring of labor comes in cooperation. The Starr County community is not generally high in this area at the moment.

Additionally, Starr County agriculture is occasionally hit by bad weather. The Christmas Freeze of 1973 devastated unharvested crops. Total market value for that year was down 9.5%.

An additional factor that has hindered development of small farm operations in Texas as in all the southwest is the struggle over water. Texas laws have changed rapidly in the past few years, and farm operators have had difficulty fitting the new laws into an operable economy. Larger operators have not fared so poorly under the new laws.

Evidence of weak community pride is that per capita retail sales is only half that of the state as a whole. Many of the cars in the Starr County supermarket parking lots are from Mexico. Many Starr County shoppers go out of the county to shop. Most go to Mission or to McAllen to shop.

Oil has been a significant, but steadily declining portion of the economy of Starr County. The continuing weak oil market has held royalties down and discouraged exploration.

Construction of businesses and residences in the county seems to be moving ahead well, but few records are kept. Although a large number of commercial centers and residences have been built in the county over the past few years, no licensed building contractors operate in the county.

The picture for the future appears to be much brighter than the picture for the past. Several development agencies are beginning to take some responsibility not only for recruiting commercial activity for the county but for building community life as well. There is evidence that some of these agencies are beginning to see the value of working together. There is also some movement to incorporate Rio Grande City before it is annexed by either Roma or La Grulla. As the strip city from Brownsville to Roma develops it will be most important to cooperate in planning and development.

A number of individuals are beginning to take it upon themselves to establish commercial activity in the county. Given the limitations of the undivided porciones and the lack of cohesive planning these persons are still committed to moving ahead. The rapid growth of the next century is an opportunity there for the taking. As the populations of Central America and Mexico reach the point of overflow, the

Brownsville < – > Rio Grande City Metropolitan Area should receive great numbers of persons who are part of these population waves. Although many of them will just be moving across the river, still they will reflect a great opportunity for entrepreneurs in industry, commerce, social services, and the Church.

Church

Starr County boasts two United Methodist Churches. St. John's Church is located several miles northwest of Rio Grande City. The congregation has a beautiful new building in an area primed for development. Although there is precious little residential area near the church site, future development should be strong in the area. The congregation, with only fifty-four members, has limited internal operations but a very strong impact on the county. Several of the members are significant business operators in the area.

The Church is also situated to be an appropriate complement to Rio Grande City First United Methodist Church. First UMC is located on a small hill above the section knows as Old Rio Grande City. With a membership of just over 200, First is a part of the Rio Grande Missionary Conference. Although First is entirely hispanic, it holds services in both English and Spanish. Mostly the elderly of the congregation participate in the Spanish services.

The original building is about sixty years old. Additional classroom space has been added to the structure. There is no off street parking available at the site. The church does operate some day care and preschool activities.

The homes in the area range from very poor to middle class. The streets are generally well maintained and driveable. The church is just a couple blocks from Main Street, a few blocks from a number of other congregations, and a few blocks from the county courthouse.

Several members of both congregations work with and support the Starr County Food Pantry in Rio Grande City. Mrs. Gigi Gutierrez is the manager of this operation which is supported by churches, individuals, businesses, the county, and various government programs. The work provides several tons of canned, frozen, and fresh food each year plus clothing and some other necessities. The churches also work together to support the local hospital.

Some estimates show a ninety per cent Roman Catholic population. This is probably vastly overstated. The actual participation figure in all congregations combined in the county is probably under thirty per cent.

The Roman Catholic Church in Rio Grande City is renovating their historic school structure at a large cost. When completed it will be usable for some of the many events that any such community needs.

A number of other congregations exist in the county in the various small communities, but none appear to be particularly important to community life. Assemblies of God, Churches of Christ and others are scattered through the county.

The primary participants in the Church Alliance are the Roman Catholics, the United Methodist Church and the Southern Baptist Church.

The primary bonding agent in the county is the extended family. Even when disputing with each other over rights to the undivided porciones families are known to support each other against other threats. These extended families typically extend along both sides of the Rio Grande River, bringing tight the international culture and relationships.

General

Very few areas of the United States have the history both of graciousness and charm and of intrigue and international participation as does Starr County. I was constantly amazed by the obvious good intentions displayed to visitors from persons in all walks of life.

The operation of the La Borde House is a case in point. Unrented rooms are left open so the guest may look around and choose which room might be the most attractive or the most comfortable for one's taste.

One highly visible aspect of this county is its acute participation in Mexican life and economics. I heard several deep, obviously knowing, discussions of the political and economic climate of Mexico as compared with Washington and Wall Street. These are some of the most experienced persons in the world when it comes to handling international transactions with diplomacy. This is probably also a contributory factor in the drug traffic.

The various groups now beginning to look for economic development are really yet in their infancy, but they will be more effective with experience. The State is providing some assistance but, as everywhere, the primary economic development must and will come from within the county.

The development of the maquilladora (twin plant) system is beginning to affect the economy of Starr County. The benefits are this plan are strong, but not strong enough to deter various American labor unions from strong objection.

As with most of the other counties of this study, two industries stand out as likely candidates for development. The first is tourism, the second is retirement. This is a marvelous area for both.

Camera buffs will be delighted with Old Rio Grande City and the easy access to Mexico. The three bridges across the Rio Grande River all lend themselves to being gateways to fascinating tours, industries, customs, and enlightenment. The bridges are thongs that hold the little international community together rather than separate it, Mexico from the United States.

Starr, Texas   Trend Information
Population and Households

	1970	1980	% Chg	1986	% Chg	1991	% Chg
	Census	Census	70-80	(Est.)	80-86	(Proj.)	86-91
Population	17707	27266	54.0	34488	26.5	40438	17.3
Households	4111	6858	66.8	8962	30.7	10812	20.6
Household Size	4.29*	3.94	-8.1	3.82	-3.0	3.72	-2.7
Group Quarters	218	218	0.0	218	0.0		
Income							
	1969	1979	% Chg	1986	% Chg	1991	% Chg
	Census	Census	69-79	(Est.)	79-86	Proj.	86-91
Agg. Income($mm)	19.9	72.7	265.8	116.8	60.6	161.9	38.6
Per Capita ($)	1123	2668	137.6	3388	27.0	4004	18.2
Average Hh ($)	4828	10635	120.3	13097	23.1	15065	15.0
Median Hh ($)	4770	7657	60.5	10226	33.6	11761	15.0
Household	Income	Distribution					
	1979		1986		1991		
	Count	%	Count	%	Count	%	
Less than $ 7,500	3387	49.4	3556	39.7	3691	34.1	
$ 7,500 - $14,999	1817	26.5	2545	28.4	3019	27.9	
$15,000 - $24,999	1090	15.9	1608	17.9	2116	19.6	
$25,000 - $34,999	303	4.4	718	8.0	1040	9.6	
$35,000 - $49,999	189	2.8	312	3.5	571	5.3	
$50,000 - $74,999	47	0.7	163	1.8	241	2.2	
$75,000 and over	25	0.4	60	0.7	134	1.2	

*1970 Household Size Is an Estimate Based on 1970 Census Data.
Data on Income Are Expressed in "Current" Dollars for Each Respective Year.
Hh=household   Agg=aggregate

Zavala, Texas
County Seat: Crystal City

Geography

At first glance Zavala County is a quiet farming and ranching county one county removed from the Rio Grande River south and west of San Antonio. It is a county of clean fields, nice homes, some river plains, some higher grazing areas, and good roads.

The eastern and northern portions of the county are largely farmland planted in a variety of vegetables. In the central areas cattle ranches predominate, but with some center pivot irrigation rigs scattering water on dry crops. One notices few cattle, although the fences and the barns would lead you to believe the cattle are around somewhere. Most of the soil in the central and western portions of the county is untillable, suitable only for livestock.

The land in the central portion is slightly elevated and rolling. The river plains are wide and flat, and appear very productive.

Crystal City is a well-designed community with a new city hall, a new courthouse, a new school, a new (and still growing) low income housing project, new fire equipment, new city park, new highway bypass around the community, and another new city street that is four lanes plus left turn lane plus parking lanes on each side that runs about a half mile, connecting Main Street with the Texas State Employment Commission office.

Batesville and La Pryor are small communities that exist to serve the farming areas along US 57, the main highway between Eagle Pass and San Antonio. These villages offer basic shopping, a decent residential area, and community pride. They also offer a real separation from the problems of Crystal City.

Population

The population of Zavala County is 90% Hispanic. Some in the county say this ratio is growing, although this is not documented. Seventy-five percent of the population was born in Texas. In the U.S., only sixty three percent of the population live in the state in which they were born.

The schools in Crystal City are almost entirely Hispanic in both staff and students. Several years ago part of the northern half of the county chose to annex their area to the Uvalde School district in the next county north rather than participate in a unitary county school system. The La Pryor area continues to support its own school, and there is a private school system built around a Baptist Church in Crystal City.

Both the marriage and divorce rates in Zavala County are below the national averages. The crime rate is about one-fourth the national average.

History

Zavala County and its current economic problems must be seen in the light of its history, particularly the history of the last thirty years or so.

Zavala County has been a habitation for hunters and trappers and fish eating people as long as humans have been in the area. The rivers and streams have provided good cover for a variety of game and for the people who have eaten them.

Before the time of Christ the civilization we know as the Aztecs were building their great civilization, and most of the Rio Grande drainage was included as part of their homeland. The Aztecs in the area of Zavala County began to be displaced by the Europeans in the 17th century.

At the close of the Mexican American war the ownership of the land was changed drastically. Some was simply grabbed by a variety of individuals, companies, and agencies. Other portions were bought up by already wealthy Hispanics. Over the years a system built up wherein a handful of land holders controlled almost the entire county.

The economy became one of vegetables for east coast tables, especially shipped through the winter when other production areas were unable to brow crops. With the development of mechanical methods of harvesting, soaring prices of energy for water for the crops, and the development of frozen food techniques for preservation, the fresh vegetable market all but dried up completely.

This series of events left, in the county, a large population of persons unable to find employment in the old ways. the more ambitious of the population had always left the Rio Grande River Valley to travel north for work in the summer. As the vegetable market in the area dried up, many of these ambitious workers chose to not return to the area for the winter. They settled in Minnesota and Iowa and Washington and other northern states to make their living.

Those who left the area permanently did not remain in agricultural field labor. Most seem to have found employment in other work. Migrant labor has largely become a thing of the past in spite of an increasing need for agricultural field workers in certain crops. With recent federal restrictions on immigration patterns and employment practices, many crops now rot in the fields for want of laborers.

With the changing economic climate of Zavala County, a new chapter of history began. Utilizing the leadership of some workers who came into the area under the sponsorship of several federal anti-poverty programs, a group call La Rosa Unida rose up to challenge the status of economics, education, social services, and potential of Zavala County.

Beginning with several of the school system staff, La Raza Unida began building a base of support for a work that eventually appeared to be moving toward the collectivization of the county.

Under the guidance of Mr. Angel Gutierrez, La Raza Unida leaders were able to marshal enough political support to be elected as school district trustees. In succeeding years, some of the La Raza Unida were elected as county and city officials as well, to the point that La Raza Unida was in virtual command of all systems in the county save those that existed at La Pryor and Batesville.

With control of the county offices in hand, La Raza Unida set about tackling the remodeling of the economic framework of Zavala County. Several steps were begun. A hog raising project on the "Heifer Project" model was initiated, although it failed within a few months.

Various state and federal grants were pursued by La Raza Unida which provided almost all the funds for such projects as the super highway, city hall, county courthouse, school buildings, and some other work. Social services delivery systems were greatly improved, and housing for low income persons was begun. The county now has more low income housing capability than is needed, and is building more.

Most importantly, and certainly most important to understanding the current economic difficulty of Zavala County, La Raza Unida chose to pursue a goal that appears to have been the collectivization of the economy of the county. The apparent goals, as stated in the grant application for a Community Development Corporation, was to bring under one roof the control of the entire economy of Zavala County. It was assumed that this would provide the framework for spreading the great wealth of the county out to a larger number of persons.

Several factors appear to have brought about the downfall of La Raza Unida in this undertaking. First, no one likes to lose either their land or their business to a government entity, and it is clear in the documents that both would have been the case. Some persons believe that these attempts would have been found illegal had they been attempted, but little is made of that aspect.

Second, the leadership of La Raza Unida had little administrative experience and almost no understanding of profit making industries.

Three, long time Hispanic middle class business people in the county began to fear for their businesses and farms in the push of La Raza Unida action.

Four, several of the leadership of La Raza Unida began to feel that they could do better personally by using their own education to go into private business or to work for a government agency themselves. People change after about ten years or so.

Eventually some non-La Raza Unida Hispanics and some Anglos have been returned to office, and tempers have cooled considerably. The turmoil of the period, though, lives on in the relationships within the community. Elections are still won and lost on La Rosa Unida-related issues.

The Crystal City school system is almost totally Hispanic: students, staff, and trustees. Some Anglo and Hispanic students attend a private school in Crystal City. Other Anglo and many Hispanic students commute to Corrizo Springs to school. Some Hispanics say this is largely a protest against bilingual education. La Pryor has its own system, and the residents of the Batesville School District have chosen to be a part of the Uvalde System in the next county rather than be a part of a La Raza Unida dominated county system.

Bilingual education is one of the symbols of the continuing confrontation. It is largely rejected by the Hispanics in the area who have middle class values. Their claim is that English is the language of the country, and they want their children educated in a language that will enable them to get ahead in business, government, and industry. "Besides," says one,"I am not a European Spaniard. The Aztecs are my people."

Economy

With the loss of thousands of people when farm labor was transformed to a lost art, many of the local stores closed. In addition, store owners began to fear the collectivization of their businesses or higher taxes, and either moved from the area to do business or just chose bankruptcy and left town.

In any case, lots of stores closed and are still closed. In addition, the development of a bypass around the community on each end of Main Street makes it very easy to live in the community, shopping in Corrizo Springs or Uvalde, and never drive down Main Street. Few cars actually make their way the entire length of Main Street.

The county economy currently is reliant on the remains of the vegetable market, and especially on the Laffere Farms of Batesville and the Del Monte plant in Crystal City. Laffere Farms produces high quality vegetables year round that are shipped north. Hard work, good employees, and a constant tending of the market are credited with the success of the Laffere family, long time United Methodists.

The Del Monte plant (California Packing Co.) relies mostly on crops brought in from other counties. Not enough is now grown in the county to satisfy production needs. It also relies on recruited labor from Corrizo Springs. Most of its managerial and supervisory personnel reside in Corrizo Springs.

Because the county has developed a highly sophisticated social services delivery system, the area would make a good low income retirement area. Living costs are low, services are excellent, and climate is superb for year round golf, fishing, hunting, and outdoor living. The development of multiple unit retirement housing along the rivers would provide excellent conditions for retirement.

Church

There are now three United Methodist congregations in Zavala County. Two Anglo congregations, at Crystal City and La Pryor, are served by the same pastor. The Hispanic congregation at Crystal City has its own pastor, and is part of the Rio Grande Conference.

All three congregations are small, each with less than 100 in attendance on any Sunday. The three seem to work together, sharing special programs, participation in community affairs, and support on special occasions. The Anglo congregation had its private academy develop during the La Raza Unida period, as did the Baptist Church across town. However that program has all but disappeared, and the Baptist program is nearly gone.

In Zavala County both congregations are hurting, and both pastors were moved this year. It appears to me that both were moved as a response to community poverty rather than any strong positive need. Both pastors were recognized by the community as community leaders. Both pastors have the reputations of being supportive community workers.

The county officials with whom I spoke (county judge, county extension agent, recorder, etc.) seemed genuinely disappointed at the moves. It seems that the two pastors were the driving force behind some much-needed self-help groups within the county, including child protection and drug abuse treatment programs.

Neither pastor wanted to move. It appears that the moves are as much the result of attempts to deal with economic frustrations as anything. This may or may not be a typical systemic response to poverty. There is also a good bit of anti-denominational feeling left from the days of La Raza Unida which may have been played out in the pastor parish relations committees.

This feeling seems to be a bit deeper in the Spanish community than the Mexican or Anglo communities. The Anglo community may have dealt with their frustrations fairly well by just being able to say that it was wrong and they were powerless to do anything about it.

The Mexican community was the power base of the La Raza Unida group, but the old-line Spanish community seems to have been largely traumatized by those years. As one lady in the town's prime restaurant told me, "We were just getting to the point we could have some property, and those ___s came in and tried to take ours with the Anglo's."

It is generally charged that this was done with the full support of the General Board of Global Ministries of the United Methodist Church. The charge is probably quite accurate. Through the 1970's and 1980's the Board threw its weight around with reckless abandon, tilting at windmill after windmill in its drive to restore judicial chivalry to an oppressive system.

Zavala, Texas   Trend Information
Population and Households

	1970	1980	% Chg	1986	% Chg	1991	% Chg
	Census	Census	70-80	(Est.)	80-86	Proj.	86-91
Population	11370	11666	2.6	12268	5.2	12748	3.9
Households	2686	3068	14.2	3327	8.4	3554	6.8
Household Size	4.22*	3.80	-9.9	3.69	-3.0	3.59	-2.7
Group Quarters	3	3	0.0	3	0.0		
Income	1969	1979	% Chg	1986	% Chg	1991	% Chg
	Census	Census	69-79	(Est.)	79-86	(Proj.)	86-91
Agg. Income($mm)	15.3	37.4	143.9	54.0	44.6	65.5	21.2
Per Capita ($)	1347	3202	137.7	4403	37.5	5137	16.7
Average Hh ($)	5691	11748	106.4	15588	32.7	17656	13.3
Median Hh ($)	4972	9242	85.9	12288	33.0	13753	11.9

Household	Income	Distribution					
	1979		1986		1991		
	Count	%	Count	%	Count	%	
Less than $ 7,500	1313	42.8	1057	31.8	985	27.7	
$ 7,500 - $14,999	954	31.1	950	28.6	950	26.7	
$15,000 - $24,999	516	16.8	723	21.7	800	22.5	
$25,000 - $34,999	189	6.2	329	9.9	420	11.8	
$35,000 - $49,999	69	2.2	189	5.7	258	7.3	
$50,000 - $74,999	15	0.5	58	1.7	104	2.9	
$75,000 and over	12	0.4	21	0.6	37	1.0	

*1970 Household Size Is an Estimate Based on 1970 Census Data.
Data on Income Are Expressed in "Current" Dollars for Each Respective Year.
Hh=household   Agg =aggregate

Black American

When the list of counties to study came to me, I was quite surprised. I had expected there to be a larger contingent of Black American counties in the deep south. Having lived in Georgia for several years, my sense was that that was where the real poverty could be found.

However, the list only produced three among the bottom twenty five. Lee, in Arkansas, with Tunica and Jefferson in Mississippi. Upon checking, several other counties in the area would usually have been on the list, but for one reason or another were absent from those assigned me to study this particular year. Most peculiar was the sense that these three are probably the most politically turbulent Black counties recently.

These three counties have all been in the news often over the past quarter century or so. Jefferson County is the home of the Evers brothers, Medgar and Charles, of civil rights unrest fame. Much civil rights activity has taken place within that county.

Tunica seems to get more than its share of political visitors. I suspect the reason to be the good airport at Memphis, only about thirty minutes from the town of Tunica itself. Politicians are tempted to come in, look at the poverty, make some hasty (and often ill advised statements) and beat a hasty retreat to go visit Graceland. Jesse Jackson has done this a time or two. His nationally recognized comments on Sugar Ditch, for instance, are as resented by the Black population of Tunica as by the Anglo population.

Lee County, Arkansas, is just across the river from Tunica. Lee's claim to fame, apart from its poverty, is that several of its prime youth migrated to Detroit. There they hooked up together in a drug ring that brought even more hurt to their home community. The jailing or death of several of these young men in Detroit has hit the community as hard as the Watts riots hit Los Angeles.

Yet with all their sadness and poverty, it is difficult to find in all the land three prettier pieces of real estate than these three counties snuggled up to the Mississippi River. The majestically contoured fields, the wooded levees and banks, the comfortable ponds give a sense of grace and dignity that is a pleasure to the eyes. Certainly no highway in American is more gorgeous to drive than the Natchez Trace.

There are certainly no friendlier people on earth unless these people feel threatened by an outsider. Everywhere we went we were treated like royalty. I believe this to be the case because we came offering hope for the future without excessive condemnation of the past.

Why are they poor? There are a thousand answers, none of them simple. Slavery, illiteracy, greed, climate, politics, etc... etc... The list can go on and on. Yet like the others, their time will come, I am convinced.

Jefferson, Mississippi
County Seat: Fayette

Few areas in the United States stand out as areas of natural beauty and economic struggle as does the Mississippi Delta country. A major symbol of both is Jefferson County, with Fayette as the county seat.

Jefferson County lies near the southern terminus of the Natchez trace. Rising from the Mississippi river elevation, the first few miles of fertile river plain is some of the richest soil in the country. The soil is high acid content, suited to a variety of crops including cotton, soy beans, and many vegetables. Several miles of hilly areas rise from the river plains, and taper off into more farmland in the eastern areas of the county. The hills are tree covered with patches of open land available for small farming operations and grazing.

US Highway 61 cuts through the county, frequently through kudzu that seems to create a green tunnel as it hangs from spreading trees on both sides of the highway. Highway 61 is being slowly transformed into a four lane super highway, but there is still enough tunneling kudzu to make photographers drool.

Fayette is about halfway between New Orleans and Memphis, two of the major cities linked by US 61. Just 30 miles north of Natchez, the county appears to not really be isolated in any real sense of the word. Although no trains operate in Jefferson County, rail service is available at Roxie and Natchez. Truck traffic is plentiful, and bus service through the area is steady. Natchez offers commuter airline service.

Alcorn A. & M. University, just across the Claiborne County line, is a modern, important university. The campus spreads over the rolling terrain with a gentle flair that belies its real economic importance to the Delta people.

History

Jefferson County has been in the news several times during the last 40 years as a stronghold of civil rights work. Charles Evers is again the mayor of Fayette. His brother, Medgar, lost his life in the struggle several years ago. Some of the loudest and strongest discussions of the place of civil rights in American society have occurred in and concerning the Jefferson County arena.

During "slavey days" the river bottom land was strong plantation area. The course of the river has changed somewhat, so some of the plantation outlines are not easy to decipher at this date.

After the Civil War, the land eventually became settled by sharecroppers and, still later, tenant farmers. However, with the mechanization of farming and the weakening of the cotton market, larger farms are back in style but without the massive numbers of persons needed to operate the plantation, sharecropper, and tenant farmer systems.

The persons displaced as the remnants of the tenant farmers system, about 60% of whom were black, were unable to find immediate work in the county. Massive poverty was the result. Some of the most difficult confrontations between black and white populations came as a high percentage of people turned to any means available to compete for the few jobs and community status symbols around. Competition by any means available was literally a life and death struggle.

Jefferson County, caught in this kind of turmoil, was not an attractive locale for the establishment of any kind of industry. The cycle of weak economy and community turmoil turned away many of the industries that might have been able, earlier on, to alleviate the economic distress.

Eventually, after some of the strongest turmoil the nation has seen, the county began both to come to grips with the issues and to gain a sympathetic ear from outside economic sources. Some industries began to establish operations in the area. Some local businesses began to succeed, if not prosper. Some of the old patterns of hostility began to disappear, and the county appears to be on its way to becoming an attractive target for a variety of economic improvements.

Because over 80% of the population of Jefferson County is Black, there was much speculation that a massive realignment of the power structures, property ownership, and economic base of the county. However, there is a strong sense that the re- alignment that has come has been along lines of general respect in the community and personalities rather than along racial lines. Person after person in Fayette speaks of the continued breaking down of racial barriers as a sign of the eventual successful recovery within the county. Many racial barriers still exist, but their influence seems to be weakening.

One woman noted that there is little to distinguish between homes of the white population of the county and the homes of the black population. She noted it is impossible to drive around and state that, by the location or appearance, `this is the home of a white family, and that is the home of a black family'.

Economy

Jefferson County has been the target of state and federally sponsored economic development activity for some time. Although the county has a very low per capita income, a number of jobs have been developed in the area over the past several years. Shifting economic forces in the world cause some of these jobs to be transient, however. Jobs come and go with world market conditions.

Much of the low per capita income statistics may be traced to the inability to develop an alternative economy for the thousands of displaced persons after the change from the tenant farmer system to a highly mechanized corporate farm structure. Many of these persons are still in the county, having been either unable or unwilling to either leave or locate employment in the area. Who can blame them for an unwillingness to leave? The Delta climate is mild and pleasant, the scenery is dramatic, social services and medical care are excellent, and the area boasts a low cost of living.

Jefferson County is one of 25 areas in the state certified to operate as "enterprise zones", areas in which new industry is entitled to a variety of tax incentives and special consideration from state and local agencies. Mississippi State income tax credits up to $1,000 annually for a ten year period may be granted, and there is a state sales tax abatement for the purchase of new machinery for manufacturing processes.

ITT and Jeffco operate plants in the county which produce wiring harnesses for automobiles. There is also a sawmill which cuts dimension lumber for furniture. Several small pulpwood companies provide added employment and income.

Wood products remain a top potential for Jefferson County. Many of the southern hardwood forests have been cleared in favor of faster growing Super Pine plantings. Because a large part of the forested land in the South is in private ownership, their products are not under the control of either the US Forest Service or state forestry units, and plantings typically consist of those trees which will make the quickest return on the investment.

Hardwood trees, on the other hand, grow slower, and are not in demand for high-volume construction. Rather, these woods are prized for furniture, carvings, utensils, and specialty applications. The land of Jefferson County has a good soil makeup for hardwoods as well as softwoods.

Other agricultural economies are practiced in Jefferson County that have some possibilities for future growth.

Cattle, especially crossbreeds using a Brahma cross, seem to do well in the county. The good grazing opportunities, together with a generally high nutrient level in some of the local hay crops, offer the possibility of low cost cattle production. However, in recent years (since the weakening of the cotton market and the demise of the tenant farmer and sharecropper systems) the return to the farmer for cattle production has not been high enough to encourage development of this as a major economic alternative.

The production of a variety of vegetable crops and innovative methods of small-lot agriculture seems to offer good potential. Alcorn A&M University, just across the line into Claiborne County, is a leader in developmental studies of vegetables and fruits which might be grown in the Delta to bring a stronger economy.

Dr. Charles Tillman, Department Chairman, and Dr. Suresh C. Tiwari, Soils Specialist, and other persons at the Department of Agriculture at Alcorn A&M, are working to develop a number of crops.

The School is particularly encouraged by the potential of Malabari Spinach, which grows exceedingly fast and thrives in temperatures over 100 degrees fahrenheit. Temperatures up to 130 degrees seem acceptable. Malabari spinach, when planted between rows of tomatoes, appears to stop a common tomato pest, mosaic virus. It is also higher in calcium and potassium than ordinary garden spinach.

In addition, grapes, blueberries, blackberries, and muscadines appear to hold good promise in the Delta. The grapes and muscadines appear to need artificial stimuli in order to develop appropriate sugar content. These crops require cool nights just before harvest to stimulate sugar content, and cool nights in July and August are not available in the Delta.

In general, semitropical fruits and vegetables hold promise of being developed for production in this area. Of crops grown elsewhere in the United States, cabbage, sweet corn, field peas, apples and peaches seem likely possibilities. Various herbs do well in the area, and amaranthus seems realistic if a market can be developed. The primary handicap in this area is that the warm, humid climate breeds many diseases and other pests that limit the value of crops.

The work at Alcorn A&M centers around the genetic adaptation of various plants to various soil, weather, disease control, and market conditions of the Delta. Because previous generations have been somewhat sociologically isolated from the rest of the nation, markets for Delta products have not been developed as extensively as has the potential of the Delta to produce these products.

Some of the land in the county with better drainage produces excellent crops of Irish potatoes. Some farmers are growing potatoes for processing by the Frito-Lay plant in Jackson. With irrigation, two crops of potatoes per year are possible in the low areas of the county.

Farming, however, remains a risky operation. Murdock Taylor, Jefferson County Assessor and Tax Collector, notes that farm land in the county has lost one third of its cash value in the last three years. Mrs. A.D. Ballard, City Clerk of Fayette and a candidate for Mr. Taylor's office, suggested that a marketing cooperative for locally grown vegetables might be very productive for the economy.

No one in the county with whom we spoke seemed ready to state that current racial prejudice is a heavy contributor to economic hardship except in the difficulty of creating a community cohesiveness in moving toward a stronger financial base. Albert Johnson, Director of Admissions at Alcorn A&M, points out that Black persons have perhaps a larger fear of failure. This fear may arise out of centuries of being told that Black persons would fail. However, Mr. Johnson notes that this fear is a universal human trait.

Albert Johnson is also the manager of Economic Development, Inc. This organization brought together 250 persons for an Economic Summit for Southwest Mississippi in May, 1987. This seminar/workshop/trade show lifted up a cooperative approach to economic revitalization in the area.

Downtown Fayette shows many commercial properties that have been abandoned in the last twenty years. Many of these have been abandoned because the population of the county has shrunk dramatically. Others have been abandoned as the business outgrew the facility.

The Medgar Evers Community Center is the site for much community action and social service programs. Senior programs, literacy programs, LIEAP, and other programs where many are brought together at once are generally handled at this facility just north of town. The County Courthouse burned to the ground recently, so the availability of the Community Center has allowed the county to make a shift in its operation from office-visit orientation to service-delivery-on-site operation.

Church

There are between 65 and 70 churches in the county, nearly all of them small. There are five Black and two White United Methodist, one Episcopal, three Presbyterian, one Roman Catholic, and approximately fifty of various Baptist groups. Other groups represented include Christ of Christ, Church of God in Christ, Church of the Light, and others.

The White United Methodist Churches in the community, First and Community, offer ministries that, while small, have significant impact on the community. Several of the county and city officials and business persons participate in that congregation. Although the congregations have shrunk dramatically with the population of the county, still they work to carry out their mission of spiritual development and support.

The Black United Methodist Churches (Adams Chapel, Hickory Block, Crown Point, Bell Hill, and Mt. Pleasant) are all small. The attendance in each runs about 15-20 persons at each of their semi-monthly services. Each congregations holds its own annual Revival services, most offer vacation Bible schools, and all have Women's groups. Most offer church school programs, and have special programs at Easter and Christmas time.

Adams Chapel regularly raises money to benefit a kidney dialysis machine program needed by some in the community. They also have special singing services 2-3 times per month.

All the Black United Methodist Churches operate on incomes of less than $10,000 per year per church.

In discussing the problems of the churches, the largest problems mentioned are lack of communication and the frustration of seeing the congregations shrink as the population dwindles in the county. All seem to share this.

Ms. Pat Queen, of Adams Chapel, says "we all have money problems. We really want to put more money in the church, but we just don't have it. The church does so much in the community with what little we have, but we would like to do a lot more. Maybe someone could show us how. We help everybody we can.'

The really positive note about the congregations, both Black and White, comes with the discussion of the impact both on personal lives and on the corporate life of the community.

"I come to church because I get a hope that tomorrow will be a better day because of my faith. Many face hardships and disappointments in our little churches. What gives us hope? Maybe I am down when I hear the sermon, but doing what the minister says picks a person up. I listen, and then I go back and read the lessons for the day. Then I have hope."

"We celebrate when the pastor returns after Annual Conference. We are always afraid we will lose our pastor. When that happens, it is terribly hard on everyone."

"I can tell the people who are close to Jesus. They just act a little nicer than those who aren't."

The Reverend Dwight Prowell, pastor at Adams Chapel and Mount Pleasant and member of the Fayette Chamber of Commerce, is concerned with the uncertainty of the future of the congregations in the light of dwindling populations. That is one of the reasons for his involvement with the Chamber of Commerce.

The congregation carries out a variety of ministries intended to help motivate persons to help themselves. Members of the churches work with families to help them understand and make use of social services available. The families are helped with budgets, planning menus, etc. Occasionally when persons need gas money to travel to a job, the churches try to help.

One particularly important ministry concept of the congregations is team visits. Persons from the congregations go to the homes of elderly, handicapped, newcomers, and others. In the homes, the team sings, gives communion, reads the scriptures, teaches a church school lesson, or does whatever is needed at that home. Most importantly, they leave the clear expectation that someone will come again to that home in the Name of Christ.

The Episcopal congregation in the community has the reputation of being the only integrated congregation in the area.

General

The most frequently repeated comment we heard in Jefferson County was that, while there is some way to go in bringing real community between the races, great strides have been made. People are willing to credit this to a variety of sources, including the churches, government programs, industrial investment, schools, (especially Alcorn A&M), and elected officials of the area. The improvement in interracial communications and community is a major source of community pride.

Several spoke of their frustration with the continued segregation of the churches in the community, and talked of several possible ways to move this process along in a very positive way. One certainty which the churches of Jefferson county face is the continuing decline of population. Unless dramatic industrial or commercial development occurs, the county will probably decline to a population plateau of about 5,000 or 6,000 persons until the residential areas of Natchez begin to spill over into Jefferson County.

Part of this decline will come as persons become more certain of their ability to leave the area and find jobs elsewhere. Other portions will be attributable to death and smaller families. In dealing with the low self image and high birth rates of the community, some of the congregations will be forcing themselves into smaller operations; working themselves out of jobs, as it were.

With such a population, churches will either be forced to merge or learn to exist on extremely limited finances and memberships. Currently existing congregations, unless some should close or merge soon, will see themselves with a maximum of 100 persons per congregation in the total population.

Perhaps the most hopeful event of our visit to Fayette was our visits with Murdock Taylor and Mrs. A.D. Ballard. Mr. Taylor is retiring, and Mrs. Ballard is one of five candidates for his office. Both of them saw the primary issue of the campaign for Jefferson County Assessor and Tax Collector as a question of personal qualifications, experience, honesty, and personality, the cornerstones of civilization.

Mrs. Ballard was comfortable with the service rendered by Mr. Taylor, and Mr. Taylor was comfortable with the caliber of persons running for his office. Because Mr. Taylor is White and Mrs. Ballard is Black, this relationship represents what the residents of Jefferson County want the world to understand as the "New Delta Community".

Jefferson, Mississippi   Trend Information

Population and Households

	1970	1980	% Chg	1986	% Chg	1991 Chg	%
	Census	Census	70-80	(Est.)	80-86	(Proj.)	86-91
Population	9295	9181	-1.2	8642	-5.9	8179	-5.4
Households	2422	2775	14.6	2692	-3.0	2617	-2.8
Household Size	3.83*	3.30	-13.7	3.20	-3.0	3.12	-2.7
Group Quarters	15	15	0.0	15	0.0		
Income	1969	1979	% Chg	1986	% Chg	1991 Chg	%
	Census	Census	69-79	(Est.)	79-86	(Proj.)	86-91
Agg. Income($mm)	9.1	29.9	228.4	38.1	27.2	41.7	9.5
Per Capita ($)	981	3262	232.5	4407	35.1	5099	15.7
Average Hh ($)	3758	10625	182.7	13910	30.9	15664	12.6
Median Hh ($)	4298	7386	71.8	10769	45.8	12107	12.4
Household	Income	Distribution					
	1979		1986		1991		
	Count	%	Count	%	Count	%	
Less than $ 7,500	1412	50.9	1033	38.4	881	33.7	
$ 7,500 - $14,999	632	22.8	718	26.7	696	26.6	
$15,000 - $24,999	496	17.9	462	17.2	477	18.2	
$25,000 - $34,999	153	5.5	288	10.7	285	10.9	
$35,000 - $49,999	71	2.6	133	4.9	190	7.3	
$50,000 - $74,999	9	0.3	52	1.9	69	2.6	
$75,000 and over	2	0.1	6	0.2	19	0.7	

*1970 Household Size Is an Estimate Based on 1970 Census Data.
Data on Income Are Expressed in "Current" Dollars for Each Respective Year.
Hh=household   Agg=aggregate

Tunica, Mississippi
County Seat: Tunica

Geography

Tunica County nestles prettily along the Mississippi river some 30 miles south of Memphis, Tennessee. Highway 61 runs north and south through the county, providing an improving access to Memphis and to Clarksdale. Both cities provide business competition and jobs for Tunica County residents. The Helena, Arkansas, community also actively competes for Tunica County money.

The Mississippi River may provide some economic strength for the community once again. Every community along the river from New Orleans north as far as the river is navigable either has a shipping port, has one under construction, or has a group of people attempting to obtain federal funding for such a project. Obviously not all of these proposed projects are warranted, but some will be completed.

The River is itself a great long farming area, producing enormous quantities of fish for the rapidly developing American taste for catfish and other slackwater fish. Partly because of the availability of fish, and partly because of the pure beauty of the area, the area also has an enormous tourist potential that is largely untapped. Some local residents have said that this is due in part to distrust of outsiders by previous generations. While this sentiment may have been true, very little of this attitude continues today, especially among those persons working to develop their communities.

History

The history of Tunica County, like so much of the history of the Deep South, is a story of a frontier impacted by cotton, slavery, fierce pride, and the Bible. As the area redevelops in the light of modern technologies, modern relationships, and modern political realities, these same factors are returning to the fore, but in ways not dreamed of in previous generations.

The reliance on cotton as the primary crop for these Delta lands has been romanticized almost beyond belief, and cotton has become a symbol both of economic strength and poverty, both of independence and repression. The development of the plantation system relied on cotton. Little in the way of skill was required for the growing and harvesting of cotton. Even the sharecropper system relied on cotton because it was a crop in which every last act could be performed by hand until the cotton was delivered to the gin.

The opportunities of the gin to process the cotton made possible a rather rudimentary continuation of the slavery system, although the slaves were technically free. The gin operator and the community store owner controlled the economics of the community, and frequently they were the same person. Money paid for the cotton by the gin operator/cotton trader would be paid to the store for necessities. This in house system provided the necessities of a steady life, albeit a poor one. Often the system was rationalized by saying that the ex-slaves were uneducated and therefore could not handle money on their own. The out growths of slavery have continued to impact the community to this day, not least in the struggle of Black persons to see themselves as God's Children and People of Ultimate Worth.

But at the same time, the redevelopment of pride in self and community is being carried on in a variety of circles among all the ethnic and racial groups of

Mississippi. During the darkest days of Mississippi, many persons both in and out of the State questioned whether Mississippi would ever recover from the massive poverty, the racial tensions, and the changing economic scene. However, across the State now we see well maintained highways, new industries, strong communities, and caring and ambitious leadership making its impact felt as the State overcomes a negative self-image through hard work and the conscious establishment of new and powerful relationships.

But this work is not complete, especially as viewed by the people of Mississippi. As various persons across Mississippi were interviewed for this project, they unanimously expressed surprise that only two of Mississippi's counties were among the twenty-five counties with the lowest per capita income in the United States in 1986, and that even these counties do not rank at the bottom of the list. There seemed to be a sad expectation that Mississippi would once again rank at the bottom of another national list of some sort.

The Bible has played and continues to play an extremely important role in the life of the Mississippi Delta. It is very difficult to pin down the exact reasons for this link, but in the conversations in the area, the image of the individual as being ultimately important was mentioned time and time again. In addition, so called Christian "Characteristics" such as personal responsibility, discipline, compassion, righteousness, and ambition were frequently mentioned as being those attributes needed for economic development.

Population

As long as such records have been kept, Tunica county has been listed among those counties that have the highest percentage of Black persons in the nation. In the 1980 census that was listed at 73.04%, compared with 35.19% in the State and 11.69% in the nation.

The Black population is at a point that it can readily control the political structure of the county. Black persons could be in control of all public offices if that were the desire of the Black population. However, such an event has not occurred, although many of the elected officials are Black. In spite of reputation, it appears that elections in Tunica County are settled on a variety of factors, but rarely on overt racial overtones.

A very important factor in understanding Tunica County is the awareness of the difficulty of women in living in the area and attempting to support a family. One of every three homes in the county is headed by a single woman, yet almost no jobs exist in the county for unskilled women. While visiting in the area, we saw three women approach persons with small businesses to ask for employment. 44% of all the households in Tunica County in 1979 were below the poverty level, but 62% of the households headed by a female were below the poverty level.

One local suggestion for the alleviation of some of these problems is the development of training programs for "live in" persons who would live at the homes of elderly or handicapped persons, or open their homes to the elderly or handicapped. There is a recurrent shortage in most areas of the nation of persons who would be willing to work this way.

Economy

There is no farmland in the United States that is prettier or richer than Mississippi Delta Farmland. For as long as humans have lived in the area the land has been a bountiful producer of a variety of crops. However, serious attempts at over-production of cotton over the last couple of centuries has left an economic blight on the community.

Cotton grows well in the Delta, especially with modern farming methods. One man, who holds some offices in the Tunica First United Methodist Church and teaches a strong adult church school class, is operating a 15,000 acre farming and processing industry of cotton and soybeans.

This man actually owns little land, but rents land from the owners at prices ranging from $40 to $80 per acre, depending on fertility, size, location, previous crops, and a variety of other factors. At one time a tenant farmer family might rent 20 acres to feed and clothe the family, a rate of about five acres per person. Now the modern corporate farmer hires about 25 persons to farm 15,000 acres. This is a rate of about 200 acres per person. Primarily for this reason, the population has shrunk from 22,000 to approximately 9,500, and the county is still heavily over populated.

Many persons who could not find or create employment in the area for themselves have been either unwilling or unable to relocate. Some are elderly, some are uneducated, some have a bit of a home in the county. The position of the county as one of the twenty-five counties in the United States with the lowest per capita income in 1986 reflects the continuing residence of many of these displaced tenant farmers. The existence of an eager labor force is a real plus for continued growth.

In l980 the total farm population for Tunica County was 670 persons, with a non-farm population of almost 9,000 persons. This data reflects a movement to the villages and the town of the population as the farmland is operated by larger operators. It was this kind of pressure on the housing systems that created the problems around Sugar Ditch. The City and County have been constructing housing for low income persons for several years as funds have become available. However, as revenue sharing packages have been withdrawn, the local governments find themselves less able to cope with the needs of the local population.

The school system is developing and building a vocational training center to enable these persons to learn the variety of skills needed to take jobs in the variety of industries now viable in the community. Farming, chemical production, agricultural processing, and tourism all require workers with specific skills. In Tunica County, the workers are there, eager to work, but they are basically untrained. The new Vocational Center should help in this area.

One employer in the county noted that cotton as a product was not the primary cause of over-reliance on the cotton industry in most of the Delta communities. Rather, he said, the self esteem and personal identity of the wealthy white population, and particularly the economically ambitious whites, centered around the plantation system with a large block of owned land, large numbers of either slaves, `free Blacks' or poor whites, and a self sufficient economy that needed only to be able to sell off a product once in a while to stay alive. Cotton fit that self image nicely, although at a large human cost. As long as the whole thing depended on the owner and family, that family got its reward even if no one made much money.

One successful farmer pointed out that "farming now is just a business". The involvement with cotton and soybeans today is an accident of geography and economics. Like any good businessman, his primary function is to make money and create a good community for himself, his family, and those around him. He spoke of the desire to provide a better life for his employees, including such things as wages, benefits, family education, and employment stability. "When my workers have a better life, I, too, have a better life."

A few White farmers are not the only successful business operators in the county. The Henderson family, starting several years ago with the family farm, have developed a wide-ranging commercial operation which includes involvement in the funeral industry, two very nice clothing stores, a janitorial chemicals packaging facility, and a distribution operation for the janitorial chemicals. Again, the Hendersons see themselves as building a better life for themselves and their community rather than as a Black family than having conquered a bad system. Peggy Henderson says "Not every problem is an obstacle, and some of our obstacles have been just plain foolishness."

James Dean is successfully building a catfish business, operating a processing and marketing set-up in Tunica as well as in Memphis, dealing with same problems as do the Hendersons and the Flowers family. "I'm not bragging, but I do serve the best catfish dinner in the Delta."

Directly across the street from Dean's Fish Market is the Blue and White Restaurant, known for its good atmosphere as well as tasty (zesty!) food. The room is typically full, and is a gathering place not only for local citizens but for tourists along Highway 61, one of the most scenic routes in the U.S.A.

As the tourist industry might develop, additional motel space will be required. "Bed and Breakfast" establishments are also needed in the county. This will ultimately produce some income for persons, particularly including some women, in service industries.

In the north end of the community, Tom Collins is developing a grocery store the hard way. With a very small stock in his living room and kitchen, and plenty of time, he makes a small but helpful income from the neighborhood. His inventory (probably under $100) pales in comparison with the larger stores in the area, and particularly with the Wal-Mart stores which are found in counties next to almost all of these poorest counties across the nation. Yet Mr. Collins, with business license on the wall next to family pictures, is effectively creating wealth for himself and other people in the county and elsewhere.

Tunica County is one of 25 areas in the state certified to operate as "enterprise zones", areas in which new industry is entitled to a variety of tax incentives and special consideration from state and local agencies. Mississippi State income tax credits up to $1,000 annually for a ten year period may be granted, and there is a state sales tax abatement for the purchase of new machinery for manufacturing processes.

Recently Tunica County received much negative publicity as one of the poorest areas of the country. Jesse Jackson came to the community and commented on one of the poorest areas of the community, an area called "Sugar Ditch" which the town of Tunica was rehabilitating at the time. Sugar Ditch was settled by ex- tenant farmers as they were moved off their lands and did not have the self-assurance to move north to where there were jobs. Most were uneducated, and few had any money. The Sugar Ditch area is low lying, and is drained by an open concrete lined ditch.

Even while the Sugar Ditch area was being settled, the town had water and sewer available at the street, but no money was available to provide sewer or water connections to the homes at city expense. In recent years the city has begun to improve the area, although much of the redevelopment has seen the residents moved to other parts of the community. The overall plan, in place for several years and simply waiting for money to become available, is intended to create a better community for those who will continue to live in the area.

One of the community leaders, Cliff Granberry, a retired liquid propane gas technician, says "I live on Sugar Ditch. My brick home is thirty feet from the ditch, and I drive a Cadillac." Granberry is a descendant of one of the earliest families in Tunica County. His grandfather was brought from Tennessee as a slave.

Granberry is part of and works with a unique organization called "Former Concerned and Concerned Citizens of Tunica" (FCCCOT). FCCCOT consists of persons, mostly Black, who have left Tunica County to make their homes and fortunes elsewhere, but wish to be supportive of their ancestral home county. FCCCOT provides scholarship opportunities for Tunica students and is looking at ways to assist in business development in the area. The group meets regularly at various places in the nation to bring back good memories and to plan good work. A current project is the development of a civic center and gymnasium for the community at a cost of some $750,000.

For a variety of reasons, including the changing agricultural scene and the development of jobs in other parts of the country, the great export of Tunica county (as most of the counties of this study) has been those persons who wished to create wealth for themselves, their families, and those around them. It appears that this has not actually been necessary in all cases, but little was done by the community to convince these persons that they could stay in the area and create their wealth.

Again, it seems to be a matter of personal and corporate identity as a community and people of poverty. The only antidote may be a development of a community image of success. I may be that a simple dream, or plan leading toward such success would be enough to prevent many of these potential makers of wealth from leaving.

Several persons, including all these mentioned here, spoke of the need to quickly develop a Chamber of Commerce in the community to lead the creation of a local cash-flow economy. Currently, surrounding communities such as Memphis, Clarksdale, and Helena both provide many of the jobs and take most of the money earned by residents of Tunica. Almost half the employed residents of the county work in other counties or states. It may be that the work of a developed Chamber of Commerce in Tunica would be most effectively centered around developing a pattern of successfully meeting the challenges of doing business in the Delta now and in the future.

With the support of the State of Mississippi, the county has developed several "Key Community Teams" which are prepared and authorized to make rapid commitments of sites and tax incentives toward attracting new industry to the county.

However, several persons who might be in position to participate in some of these programs seemed unaware of their potential and how to go about participating in them. The county has only recently begun to see the ways that these programs could be helpful. One person noted that because the county had not had a really good voting record, it seemed that the State of Mississippi had been unwilling to put much money into development in the County.

Currently one site is being developed as an industrial park, and others are being prepared. Low income housing is being planned and construction should begin later this year. Highway 61, which runs the length of the county, is slated for reconstruction as soon as the legislature approves. Highway 61 is a narrow but beautiful highway down the River corridor. It is one of the most beautiful highways of America although it runs through some of the most poverty stricken areas.

Church

The Church Directory page of the Tunica Times-Democrat lists forty churches in Tunica County, or one church for each 200 persons in the county. The existence of so many churches in the county once again reflects the days when over 22,000 persons lived in the county, and the Church was the center of social life, social life, and spiritual life.

The churches of Tunica County appear, at this time, to be only mildly active. Indeed, the First United Methodist Church, a "white" United Methodist Church and the only United Methodist Church in the county, is reported by some of its members to be a "Sunday Morning Only" Church. The Lane Chapel Christian Methodist Episcopal Church and the St. Peter's African Methodist Church, both of which have historically Black memberships, are small.

First United Methodist Church, however, may have an impact on the community beyond its numbers and its mid-week activities. James Wilson, the mayor of Tunica, is a member, as is Dick Flowers and several others of the community leadership.

The current pastor at Tunica First is William Lampkin. He was appointed to this charge at Annual Conference 1987. Mrs. Johnny Lampkin was appointed to the Lula-Friars' Point Charge in neighboring Coahoma County at the same time. The decision of the Reverends Lampkin to accept this appointment was based on their desire to serve neighboring pastorates, to be in situations where their ministries would have the greatest impacts on the communities, and to simply go where needed most. First Church Tunica is a rather new building, with nice furniture and a good history, and apparently good opportunity to be in mission to the community in a variety of ways.

Dave Williams, vocational education instructor at Rosa Fort High School and member of Fredonia Missionary Baptist Church, talked of the need for churches to help motivate the youth so they would stay in school, get educations, and be able to go after the available business activity in the area.

Perhaps more importantly, says Williams, the church needs to learn to operate as a responsible business in the budgeting, goal setting, programmatic, and financial processes, and teach these skills to the whole congregation. In this way both youth and adults would be prepared to develop their own businesses and pursue their own financial independence. He noted that we seem to be developing continuing generations of youth who come to adulthood without understanding what it takes to create wealth.

Other churches in the community tend to follow similar patterns of strong traditionalism, racial separation, and financial problems. It has been estimated that only about 1500 persons are in church on Sunday Morning in Tunica County. If about four of these churches account for 500 worshipers, that leaves 1,000 persons for 36 churches, or an average of less than 30 worshipers per congregation.

Small congregations can be effective, however. The Reverend Lampkin says "The United Methodist Church has the capacity to be the revitalization of Christianity in this nation. This will not be through choosing between charismatism or fundamentalism, but by good ministry on a day to day basis in all congregations. Small congregations have a real awareness of the world that is missing from the General Boards and larger groups of the Church. The small congregations have to be and are willing to deal with new ideas and programs."

Of course, it is worth noting to Lampkin that it is the General Board of Global Ministries that made a stab at understanding by sending a team to these areas in the first place.

Although Friars' Point Church is in another county, it is worth noting that this small church has a very active prison ministry. It has a searching and consistent pattern of outreach ministry which tends to include persons in rather than out. This has come about because the congregation has intentionally chosen this mission. It is the congregation that has implemented it from the heart.

General

As Tunica County is impacted more and more by Memphis growth, and a few small businesses develop in the county, and the remaining ex-tenant farmers either die or move away, the per capita income will increase rapidly. This county could well be off the list within ten years. On the other hand, the current reputation of the county as a poverty-stricken area may serve to further alienate the county from economic prosperity.

Although the state is attempting to be supportive, and is providing good service, the primary development processes will come in the motivation and training of local persons. As local available potential work forces are recruited and trained, and as the community learns to work together for the common good, the economics should become stronger.

Local self-help work groups coming together to create a stronger economy, working with outside groups such as FCCCOT and the State of Mississippi, should have in impact far beyond their numbers. The key will be in the recruiting, organizing and training of these work groups.

Local role models such as the Hendersons and the Flowers and Tommy Collins and Jimmy Dean will provide good impetus. Increased traffic from better roads will make it more feasible to work in Memphis and live in Tunica. Retirement communities are being developed along the River. The school system is taking its role as economic development trainer seriously. All together, the future looks good for Tunica, although the next several years will be painful.

Tunica, Mississippi   Trend Information
Population and Households

	1970	1980	% Chg	1986	% Chg	1991	% Chg
	Census	Census	70-80	(Est.)	80-86	(Proj.)	86-91
Population	11854	9652	-18.6	9158	-5.1	8730	-4.7
Households	3072	2814	-8.4	2751	-2.2	2694	-2.1
Household Size	3.83*	3.42	-10.6	3.32	-3.0	3.23	-2.7
Group Quarters		17	17	0.0	17	0.0	
Income							
	1969	1979	% Chg	1986	% Chg	1991	% Chg
	Census	Census	69-79	(Est.)	79-86	(Proj.)	86-91
Agg. Income($mm)	13.7	31.4	129.0	38.9	23.8	42.1	8.3
Per Capita ($)	1156	3251	181.2	4243	30.5	4820	13.6
Average Hh ($)	4439	11167	151.6	14122	26.5	15623	10.6
Median Hh ($)	4505	6637	47.3	9081	36.8	10245	12.8
Household	Income	Distribution					
	1979		1986		1991		
	Count	%	Count	%	Count	%	
Less than $ 7,500	1586	56.4	1213	44.1	1063	39.5	
$ 7,500 - $14,999	625	22.2	771	28.0	776	28.8	
$15,000 - $24,999	336	11.9	374	13.6	419	15.6	
$25,000 - $34,999	126	4.5	182	6.6	188	7.0	
$35,000 - $49,999	49	1.7	96	3.5	119	4.4	
$50,000 - $74,999	65	2.3	52	1.9	58	2.2	
$75,000 and over	27	1.0	63	2.3	71	2.6	

*1970 Household Size Is an Estimate Based on 1970 Census Data.
Data on Income Are Expressed in "Current" Dollars for Each Respective Year.
Hh=household   Agg=aggregate

Lee, Arkansas
County Seat: Marianna

Geography

Lee County is a basically flat county of some 602 square miles alongside the Mississippi River in East Central Arkansas. In 1980, 83% of all land area was in farms.

The St. Francis National Forest with Bear Creek Lake as its central drawing point, is largely contained in the south central portion of the county. Some rolling areas at various places in the county make farming difficult, but not impossible.

Located within an hour of Memphis, and within a few minutes of Forrest City, county residents have easy access to larger metropolitan areas for employment, recreation, and shopping. Because it is located directly across the Mississippi from Tunica, Mississippi, it is tied quite heavily to that community. Additionally, I spoke with many persons who had lived in both communities or had relatives on the other side of the river.

The Mississippi River and its tributaries provide good fishing and other recreation.

History

John Patterson, the first Anglo-Saxon child born just north of Marianna in what was to become the State of Arkansas, liked to proclaim "I was born in a Kingdom; raised in an Empire; attained manhood in a Territory and now am a citizen of a State". And right he was! Lee County was at one time a part of the Kingdom of Spain; then it became a part of France, and was included in the Louisiana Purchase. Arkansas was made a state in 1836.

At the beginning of the Civil Way, some 300 men went from what was later to be known as Lee County to fight on the side of the South. Most of these were lost in various battles or chose not to return to Lee County after the War. In 1873 Lee County was created from portions of four other counties and named after Robert E. Lee. At that time it had a population of about 5,000. The population in 1889 was 18,000.

During the 1960's and 1970's, Lee County was the scene of much struggle concerning civil rights. Several groups came into being in the county having full civil rights as their basic stated goal and purpose. For several reasons the struggle came just at a time the county would have been in serious turmoil anyway, and feelings ran high. School boycotts, business boycotts, and public denunciations of well intentioned people on all sides came just as the major impact of the well-documented changes in farm and industrial economy began to hit Lee County. The entire level of frustration ran to the boiling point on all sides.

Many memories of these times still set hard in the minds of a lot of people in Lee County, creating some personal struggles that appear to have a part in denying Lee County its needed economic development. Some individuals and groups have worked hard at bringing alleviation of these feelings, but it is still a major load on the community. Serious effort by several organizations may pay off in some serious economic development within a few years.

In recent months some industrial jobs have been lost to a variety of factors, including foreign competition, labor actions, and tax changes. These lost jobs call up again some of the old animosities, although racism apparently has little to do with the current issues.

Population

Like so many other areas of the Old South, the population of Lee County from the 1890's to the 1950's centered on the sharecropper and tenant farmer systems. Most of the Old South rural counties had a population of about 30-40 persons per square mile. This was enough to provide a family for about each 40 total acres of land, and about half that was not farmable.

In this period nearly all the land was in white hands, and about 40% of the sharecroppers and tenant farmers were White, and about 60% to 70% of the entire population was Black. That racial ratio holds approximately true to this day in Lee County and several others in the area.

With the demise of the old hand labor tenant farmer and sharecropper systems, 14,000 or so householder population who worked the land have been reduced to about 2,000 total required exclusively farm population total. This displacement left about 12,000 persons to find other ways to survive if they stayed in Lee County.

Many of these persons left the area in the 1950's and 1960's, creating drastic hardships on businesses built up and geared for the higher pre-mechanization population. Businesses that catered to masses of customers with even small incomes started feeling the pinch as soon as the first mechanical cotton pickers came to the county.

It is not easy to state that one event brought another, but either in part because of or in addition to this sudden over population and the poverty that came with it came the great civil rights struggles of the 1960's and 1970's. It is impossible to summarize all that went on around this issue even in one county, but certain events are still remembered as setting the stage for current economic difficulties.

With businesses struggling to stay alive and service a large newly poorer population, an economic boycott was called against the core of the town of Marianna. With schools suddenly having to lay off teachers because of lack of funds and lack of students, a boycott was called against the school system. The Douglas and Lomason plant was unionized. Shortly thereafter the work force was cut in half, their jobs sent elsewhere to non union plants or abandoned entirely.

This series of events in Lee County, beginning as the stage was set by the plantation system in the middle 1800's, has played out into a community beset by unemployment, distrust, closings, weak churches, and a general feeling in the whole community of having been betrayed by civilization itself, if not by God and the Church.

If the story ended here, it would be hard to make a case for any hope in the immediate future for Lee County. The events cited here all reached their peak about fifteen years ago, and some in the community are frustrated that not more progress has been made.

However, in Lee County several disparate voices now are beginning to make a kind of universal pitch for a next step in the process of relationships. Lon Mann (farmer and businessman, White), John Eason (clinic director, Black), W.M. Chaffin (mayor and retired Sears Personnel Manager and retired Army Captain, White) and James Turner (local executive of Delta Development, Black) all speak of the need to put old frustrations aside and work together for the development of the community. A variety of organizations is working now to deal positively with these relational needs.

Lee County will probably continue to decline in population for the next several years regardless of expanded economic frameworks. Many of the best and brightest of the young adults continue to leave the community.

This exodus is a heavy concern for James W. Banks, life long resident and very successful basketball coach. From the public high school, seven out of eight basketball players go on to college, and 67% of all high school graduates go on to college. The county high school has about 800 students.

Mr. Banks says the high motivation for education stems from the insistence at the school that education is the only way to have upward mobility of our society. He also makes two other very important points in teaching self esteem. "First, to make a contribution you must be in the world of work. Work is the nature of anyone who gives. Second, role models are essential. Our previous graduates make our best role models, so we bring them back to let the people see them whenever we can."

Troy Huddleston, who wholesales magazines in stores for Anderson News Company of Little Rock, talked about the unique buying patterns of Lee County. "People here buy good stuff. They buy Disney books, Bible stories, even the Bible itself. And a lot of Black Pride material sells. Jet, Ebony, Black Beat. Sports is only sort of average, but teen magazines do well. In one store I place 48 Harlequin Romance books every week. It's like people here are learning to like themselves. It's not like this in any other county around."

Economy

The old farm systems of the rural south created a stable, if not creative, economy for the population. As the plantations gave way to sharecropping and tenant farming, the changeover in lifestyle was really not all that much. Life went on from one generation to the next pretty much the same.

With the coming of mechanization which forced millions of families off the land they had farmed for years, a complete way of life was changed in a couple decades. Families that had identified themselves as farmers were forced to see themselves as factory workers or teachers or something else, anything but farmers. This meant, for most, moving into towns in the area or moving "up north", leaving the quiet peacefulness of rural life and entering into the forced elbow rubbing of city life. Such transition in itself is an open invitation to domestic turmoil.

Conversations within the community point to a particular portion of this reidentification process that has been most painful and that gives specific clues to the continuing economic problems of Lee County. As part of the civil rights movement it was deemed necessary to be, at times, confrontational in style. As one man said, "It was necessary that some of us would be out in the street, screaming and yelling and raising hell."

John Eason, Director of the Lee County Cooperative Clinic, noted that the unwillingness to work together was at least as strong between Black groups as between Whites and Blacks. "It may be because that's the way we made it this far."

Some of the White population carried the same kind of style, a shouting, confrontational, noisy, media grabbing style. Perhaps because of the openness of that style, caught and displayed vividly on television and in other media, many persons, both Black and White, became trained in this mode of community behavior.

In every generation there are people who seem to have the knack of creating wealth for themselves and for the people around them. These people can take a small opening in the environment, shape it and mold it, and come up with a way to make a few dollars, and in the process help others do the same. However, in most of the counties in this study, these people have left the area to go where the possibilities are better. The primary handicap of Lee County, say the people we talked to in the community, is the image of turmoil. Businesses do not fare well in communities in turmoil, so many of those who could create wealth have left.

But that legacy appears to be on the way out, and not simply because of passing years. Too many of the participants in those years of open struggle are still in the community to allow the memories to die of old age alone. Rather, it appears that the community is on the brink of bringing about community harmony in a truly remarkable way, intentionally.

The reasons for this are varied, says the community. Economic survival may be the chief reason. Another may be that the personalities involved are older now, and wiser. And another may be that some of the changes that have come in the community have been somewhat pleasant. The town has seen a state basketball championship in the single public high school, a high rate of students going on to college, improved health care, better water supplies and sewer systems, a developing Chamber of Commerce, a new Coca Cola plant.

A rather major community issue that arose as part of this whole package is one that has appeared in city after city in this study. At some point a highway bypass was built around Marianna, allowing traffic to go past the town without even slowing for it. In addition, roads were being improved to Helena, Forrest City, and Memphis. The draw of larger areas for shopping and employment and services was too much for downtown Marianna to compete. Businesses began to close downtown, and today the square is only about half occupied. Regionalization does much damage to the small town.

Because this occurred at about the same time as the other community turmoil was strongest, many blamed much of the demise of the city center on the turmoil. However, other businesses began to open along the bypass or on the streets leading to the bypass, and many of these are doing well. As both standard and low-income residences have been built in the community, these have been clustered around the bypass. The hospital and the Cooperative Clinic are near the bypass, nearly a mile from the town square.

The town square, on the other hand, with the courthouse, city hall, several businesses, and several empty buildings, is on the east side of town with its back nearly to the L'Anguille River. Chestnut Street, the primary east west arterial, runs another two blocks and ends, forming a "U" with Main street which runs back west. One would rarely go through the city square to go anywhere.

All four of the persons mentioned above as being leaders in the community (Chaffin, Turner, Mann, and Eason) are involved in activities that have as a part of their purpose the development of a positive community togetherness and consciousness. And they are not alone. Throughout the community people talked about what they are involved in that should help in this area. There exists a conscious effort to give the county an identity of togetherness and compassion to replace the old. The community hopes that as this happens the personal identification crises within the community will ease. With this improvement it is more likely that commercial development and the work of building a better county will be on course.

The county is a well diversified farming area. Cotton, rice, wheat, soybeans and grain sorghum are all well suited to Lee County. The University of Arkansas Cotton Branch Experiment Station and Soil Testing Lab are located three miles south of Marianna in the center of the county. The soil testing lab is one of the most modern in the nation, giving fast service to farmers all over the state by way of computers.

Flood irrigation in the rice fields has long been a familiar sight but now center pivot irrigation rigs irrigate many of the crops. With irrigation have come big increases in yields.

The number of cotton gins in the county has declined noticeably, but the ones that are left are high capacity plants. The Federal Compress and Warehouse in Marianna is equipped with the latest weighing, handling, and sampling equipment. Storage for over 70,000 bales is available so cotton is shipped into Marianna for storage.

Three grain elevators are located in the county and many farmers have their own storage systems for rice, wheat, and grain sorghum on their farms. A vegetable cooperative in Marianna is beginning to encourage the production of crops suited to smaller operations. Peach and pecan orchards are doing well.

One of the larger employers in Lee County is the Cooperative Clinic. This original VISTA project, a National Health Center Clinic, provides a variety of health services for the poor of the community on a $1.5 million budget. Starting as a couple doctors working out of a car, the Clinic has become both a major health service provider and a catalyst for community action. With 75-100 patients per day, the clinic operates on the personal identities of people as much as on their bodies.

John Eason, the clinic director, says Jesus would deal with the economic issues of Lee County "First, by getting people involved in helping themselves, by giving them the sense of being somebody. Second, He would bring people together both for survival and for development. We don't have a good history of working together here, but we are all trying to change that."

Church

The churches of Lee County are reported to be somewhat disconnected from the community needs. Not one person with whom we talked related any positive effort on the part of any congregation toward bringing about community harmony.

One woman was asked "What do any of the churches do that is positive for the county?"

Answer: "Nothing".

Yet this could not be entirely accurate. W.M. Chaffin and Lon Mann are members of First United Methodist Church, and as mayor and leading businessman/developer, these two impact the community as powerfully as any. It appears that the churches of the community expect that their impact on the community will be solely through the individual work of their members. But as Lon Mann said, "Sometimes it gets lonely out there, but we have to keep trying in order to survive and because it is right."

It is reported that the First Christian Church and First United Methodist Church are the strongest churches in the community of Marianna. Livingston Chapel (Black) has among its membership a number of persons who are leaders in the public school system, but it has no functional adult groups. Livingston Chapel was part of the Marianna Cooperative Parish, but that organization seems to no longer exist.

In Lee County all the churches have shrunk in size as the population of the county has shrunk. The congregations dwindled just at the time finances were going down from a shrinking economy and the input of the Church into the community was desperately needed. This must have been frustrating for the pastors of all the churches over the last quarter century. This may show up in the reported inability of the Ministerial Alliances to work together.

One of the premier difficulties of shrinking populations in county seat towns is that the churches become no longer able to pay their denominational askings, their apportionments. No matter how hard they try, they simply are unable to continue the old way of doing things and pay their rising apportionments at the same time. One pastor said, "How can we keep asking for more money from fewer people who have less and less?"

Few churches in the County of any denomination are the full time work of a single pastor. Almost every pastor either has another job, serves more than one congregation, or is semiretired. Experience in other areas has taught that this can be effective ministry as long as it is not experienced as a symbol of personal or professional lack of worth. As E.D. Davis said, "It just seems that a small church always has one foot in the grave." The reversal of that image may be very difficult in a shrinking population. Almost all Christian groups have a constant battle to avoid the numbers game when evaluating the life of the congregation.

How important is the Church in Lee County? Nearly every person we spoke with made the wish for the Church to heal the community of its hurts. This may be a very heavy load for the congregations of Lee County working alone or together, but as Edna Van Pell said, "If God won't help me when I hurt, who will?"

In the pizza parlor, as we filled our plates with good salads and luscious and gooey pieces of pizza and spoonsful of pasta, a young woman across the counter was singing quietly the little hymn,

"Bind us together, Lord;
Bind us together with cords that cannot be broken.
Bind us together, Lord;
Bind us together, Lord;
Bind us together with Love!"

Lee, Arkansas   Trend Information
Population and Households

	1970	1980	% Chg	1986	% Chg	1991	% Chg
	Census	Census	70-80	(Est.)	80-86	(Proj.)	86-91
Population	18884	15539	-17.7	15112	-2.7	14730	-2.5
Households	5199	4942	-4.9	4949	0.1	4951	0.0
Household Size	3.61*	3.11	-13.7	3.02	-2.9	2.94	-2.6
Group Quarters	150	150	0.0	150	0.0		
Income	1969	1979	% Chg	1986	% Chg	1991	% Chg
	Census	Census	69-79	(Est.)	79-86	(Proj.)	86-91
Agg. Income($mm)	27.1	53.6	97.8	70.2	31.1	79.0	12.5
Per Capita ($)	1434	3447	140.4	4645	34.8	5360	15.4
Average Hh ($)	5190	10627	104.8	13895	30.8	15603	12.3
Median Hh ($)	4747	7401	55.9	10506	42.0	11777	12.1
Household	Income		Distribution				
	1979		1986		1991		
	Count	%	Count	%	Count	%	
Less than $7,500	2501	50.6	1888	38.1	1662	33.6	
$7,500 - $14,999	1348	27.3	1446	29.2	1416	28.6	
$15,000 - $24,999	691	14.0	878	17.7	964	19.5	
$25,000 - $34,999	240	4.9	391	7.9	454	9.2	
$35,000 - $49,999	56	1.1	201	4.1	266	5.4	
$50,000 - $74,999	73	1.5	57	1.2	93	1.9	
$75,000 and over	26	0.5	74	1.5	84	1.7	

*1970 Household Size Is an Estimate Based on 1970 Census Data.
Data on Income Are Expressed in "Current" Dollars for Each Respective Year.
Hh=household   Agg=aggregate

Anglo American

The Anglo counties in the study seemed at first glance to be "just six more sets of poor folks". If all the Hispanic, all the Black, all the Native American counties could be lumped into blocks, certainly we could do the same with the Anglo (White) counties. Wrong on both counts!

Hancock, Tennessee, is an isolated hill country county. Harding, South Dakota, is hard scrabble farming. Douglas, South Dakota, is Amish. Elliott, Kentucky, is wild canyon country which used to be sheep country. Owsley, Kentucky, has coal mines and tobacco. McCreary, Kentucky, has lumber mills and a growing commercial area.

Perhaps strangely enough, it was the comparison of these Kentucky counties that forced me into some of my most difficult observations about the causes of poverty in the U.S.

The first matter that hit me was the inability of the residents to work in a focused and cooperative effort. I saw this time and again throughout the study. This is painful personally to me because it is one area the Church is uniquely fit to attack in its war on poverty and misery.

The second area also caused concern. I saw the Church literally choosing to wash its hands of these people who had no money and no hope of getting any in the foreseeable future. I literally saw devout Christians swept out of the Church because of their attempts to make a little money for themselves, their families, and their communities. I came to see that the Church sometimes views making money as sinful.

I was welcomed with open arms in all these counties. I even have been called at home by a variety of these people, wanting to give me more information or ask how the project was coming along. It was really as if they are desperate for contact with the Church. Perhaps it is just contact with the outside world that is needed. It was clear, however, that the desperate call was to the Church. This was so inspite of the reality that the Church has failed its promises so often in the past.

All three of these counties have some possibilities, especially for retirement for lower income persons. Housing, utilities, medical care are all relatively inexpensive, although medical care may be some distance away.

They are lovely people, and I feel honored to count them as my friends.

Elliott, Kentucky
County Seat: Sandy Hook
Geography

Elliott County is a county of 234 square miles about fifty miles due east of Lexington and ten miles east and south of Morehead. The county is an area of rolling hills cut by some very deep and narrow canyons. The whole county is a tribute to ancient earthquake and erosive action. Through these canyons run some of the most picturesque streams in North America.

The rough terrain has somewhat isolated Elliott County as it has made highway construction difficult and rail bed construction nearly impossible. The highways that do run through the area are routed along the ridge tops as much as possible, going down into the valleys and canyons only when necessary. Most of the residences out of Sandy Hook itself are located on ridges. This format delivers some of the most attractive "living room window views" imaginable.

The Little Sandy River passes through Elliott County from southwest to northeast. What little farmland there is focused in the river plain and on top of the surrounding ridges. In the river plain much of the land is in tobacco, while on the ridges there is more corn and hay.

A supply of coal has provided jobs in the past, but almost all that is now played out leaving only a little for local use.

History

The history of Elliott County reads as colorful and independent as are its people. A way of life has developed in Elliott County that both ties it to the rest of Eastern Kentucky and separates it. Because of the semivoluntary isolation, outsiders have often seen it as a place "not quite civilized", as one native noted. These same outsiders have often been the butt of jokes and pranks designed to give a little fun to the good old boys sitting around the tables at Percy Pennington's Frosty Freeze.

Stories of moonshining (there has been some) and abject poverty (some of that as well) and marijuana crops (same) have made their way into both the local lore and the `scholarly' reports of outsiders. The truth of the whole matter is that the current generation of people who live in Elliott County do so by thoughtful choice.

Elliott County was formed in 1869 out of parts of three other counties. It is named for Judge John M. Elliott of Bath County. Judge Elliott had been banished from the bar for his support of the Confederacy.

Because the land is quite difficult to farm, the earliest settlers were hunters and trappers. What little cropping was done was typically on plots of less than one acre. The primary agricultural product developed was a strong sheep industry, supplying lamb, mutton, and wool to a growing flatland population.

Local stories abound about the participation of county residents in the Civil War. The general theme is that the men joined up, started collecting their pay, and then stayed home doing what they have always done before fighting each other. Why go off to Ohio or Mississippi to fight the enemy over slavery when the real enemy lives on the next ridge and the issue is pretty girls and grazing rights?

After the Civil War the sheep industry grew, making Elliott County one of the leading producers in the nation. Two events, however, seemed to work together to destroy this industry. First, the western United States began to import Basque sheepherders from Europe to work the sheep at very low cost. Second, the Second World War intervened.

In WWII, many of the youth either volunteered or were drafted into the service, leaving no one to carry on the work with the sheep. In addition, it is told that the soldiers in WWII had to eat so much mutton that all the men from Elliott County swore they would never force that kind of food on anyone again. When they came back to Kentucky, they simply did away with the remainder of the sheep industry.

Following WWII, the coal industry began to develop a little as strip mining became a possibility with the huge machinery available. Although Elliott County only had a little coal, by the late 1970's a coal boom had come and gone in the county.

Apart from these events, not much has happened to focus much attention of Elliott County, and that appears to be the choice of the community. The conscious decision to live in a somewhat out of the way county has created a toughness of character, a gentleness of community spirit and an acceptance of status that helps in tough times.

Population

The population totals of Elliott County appear to be holding quite steady over the last half century except while the coal boom was in progress. From 1970 to 1980 the population grew from 5,933 to 6,908. From 1980 to 1986 the population shrank only from 6,908 to 6,902, and is expected to decline to 6,885 by 1991. This decline appears to be attributable both to the loss of the coal economy and an aging population. The State of Kentucky projects that Elliott County population will swell to 8,658 by the year 2020. This stable growth pattern is seen as a very desirable note by a large part of the population.

The average household size in the county has declined from 3.6 in 1970 to 3.01 in 1986, and is expected to reach 2.93 by 1991. This combination of factors should see the per capita income rise from $1,325 in 1969 to $5,308 in 1991, and the median household income rise from $4,907 to $12,787 over the same period.

The county is listed as having no nonwhite population, and less than 1% Spanish origin. Ninety percent of the current population was born in Kentucky. Elliott County, for all its economic woes, had a net loss of 36 persons to migration in 1984.

Economy

In 1985 the total county labor force was 1,889 persons, of whom 1,510 had employment. Fifty three persons held agricultural employment, and 1,457 nonagricultural. The unemployment rate of about 20% still holds in 1987. The largest single category of employment is local and state government.

One factor that has affected the history and the economy of Elliott County is the career of choice of many of the men. Elliott County has a reputation of producing and providing pipefitters for major construction work around the world. Few major nuclear or other steam power generation plants are built without major labor input from the pipefitters of Elliott County.

While the work is not steady, and the employment calls for the workers to be away from home for months at a time, there are some good benefits. When not on the job, the workers may be able to be at home for months at a time, living inexpensively, gardening, raising a little tobacco, building a home, getting to know one's family, and generally living a life many may only dream of.

In addition, the union benefits are helpful in taking part of the burden of being unemployed for several months. Insurance, job search, and collegiality are all essential for the good life.

Even more than the economic benefits is the matter of personal pride and identity. It is said that even during the height of the coal boom in the county many men chose to leave home to work as pipefitters rather than stay home, make as much money, and mine coal. As one said, "I am a pipefitter, not a truck driver. I do have some pride, you know." This personal pride seems to drive the county when economy fails.

Most small farms exist on tobacco supports. On a spot only a little larger than a good garden a family can bring in $3,000 - $5,000. With that little cash, a small home paid for, wood for the stove and the fireplace, and a good garden, a family can live rather comfortably, especially if one can pick up a few odd jobs in the neighborhood splitting wood, doing a little housing construction, or filling in at the gas station. Life is tight, but comfort is not impossible. With food stamps, and perhaps some unemployment insurance, living can be reasonably good.

Because of this image of the good life in Elliott County, some seemingly small changes that are ahead in the life of the county economy have more to do with personal identity than with the financial structures.

When the tobacco subsidies are finally dissolved, an entire way of life will be threatened. This will not be so much a problem in areas where the fields are large and the corporate farms can shift production to another crop. But in this area where tobacco is a matter of personal pride and identity as well as a reasonable income, moving away from the tobacco economy will be a traumatic event.

There appears to be little in the way of an economy that could satisfactorily replace tobacco financially, even ignoring the personal pride and identity issues. The soil appears to be appropriate for assorted vegetables and fruits. These do well in test plots operated by various agencies. But the financial problem is that there is no market with any substance for these vegetable crops.

Some attempts at developing marketing cooperatives for various crops in Eastern Kentucky have been made. These attempts have generally been abandoned after a short time. The failures have come in part because of the community identity as a tobacco economy. One study quoted showed a lack of personal commitment to anything other than the tobacco economy.

One attempt that has been made by the Appalachian Regional Commission and Morehead State University involves providing thirty ewes to a farmer. The farmer is then to purchase a ram, and out of the resultant flock repay the ewes in kind.

Church

The many churches of Elliott County are typically the social as well as spiritual community centers, and some are active in community development projects as well. A general good feeling of ecumenism exists in the community, although occasional doctrinal disputes bring a few stout words.

The Sandy Hook United Methodist Church seems at the moment to be the weaker of the UMC's in the county, although it has a larger attendance and higher budget. This church works at being a church, and carries out several programs to help the community and provide an adequate income for the pastor.

The congregation feels it has had no real successes for some time. The limited income of the people, together with the small size of the congregation, creates a tight financial arrangement.

The Stark United Methodist Church feels very active and successful right now in spite of its size and its isolated location. A Friday night family night and study time brings the church and community together in a somewhat more relaxed period. Leaders of the church attribute much of their tripling of attendance over the past three years to this central event of the life of the community.

The congregation programs recreational events such as evenings of ROOK, pizza parties, and volleyball. The core of the program, though, is the Friday night study, choir practice, and good time.

The congregation at Stark is now predominantly men. As opposed to both the national population figures and the denominational figures, Elliott County has more men than women, and Stark Church numbers more men in attendance on Sunday morning than women.

The Stark congregation averages about fifty persons per Sunday, making it and the Sandy Hook church two of the larger congregations in the county. The Stark congregation had seventy children enrolled in Vacation Bible School in 1987.

The first authentic evidence of the Methodist Church in Martinsburg (later named Sandy Hook) bears the date of October 9, 1886, and notes its membership at 22. The church at Stark was established at about the same time.

Another document dated 1886 lists the preaching places on the Martinsburg Circuit as Martinsburg, Walnut Grove, Wells Creek school House, McClung Chapel, Antioch, Fairview, Wimberly, Newfoundland, Shiloh, Newcomber, and Hamilton. This circuit was part of the West Virginia Conference, Catlettsburg District.

The original church at Sandy Hook was torn down and moved to where the church stands today in 1892. In 1927 a tornado destroyed the building, and the present building erected.

The Sandy Hook congregation is involved in a variety of community events besides its own morning and evening worship on Sunday, Wednesday evening Bible Study, and other meetings. The group supports the community Tobacco Festival, and school events.

General Comments

In part because of the transportation difficulties and in part because of the small number of potential votes in the county, it is said that Kentucky politics doesn't really invade the county. Several mentioned that as a "plus" for the county. Many counties in most states would love to have that distinction.

Two men of the community, both of whom have chosen to live in the county after having lived elsewhere, were asked why this was their choice. After thinking it over, they presented this list.

1. It is a good religious community, with good feelings between the churches and the various pastors.
2. There are good family ties to hold on to, and everyone takes family ties seriously.

3. Safety is an important part of life. In Elliott County everyone knows and is known by everyone else.
4. There is a minimum of drug traffic in the county.
5. Wild deer and turkey make good hunting both for food and for recreation.
6. There are many truly wild places to go, places where you might stay a year and not see another human being.
7. It's a good place to raise children. We are all family here.
8. Elliott County has a slightly slower pace than some larger communities. "We are not overly formal."
9. It is a cosmopolitan community. A large percentage of the community has traveled abroad for education or for pleasure or for business. There are probably as high a percentage of persons with passports in Elliott County as any county in the nation.
10. There is no class separation. "We're all broke. Ha! Ha! Ha!"

Elliott,Kentucky   Trend Information
Population and Households

	1970	1980	% Chg	1986	% Chg	1991	% Chg
	Census	Census	70-80	(Est.)	80-86	(Proj.)	86-91
Population	5933	6908	16.4	6902	-0.1	6885	-0.2
Households	1646	2223	35.1	2290	3.0	2349	2.6
Household Size	3.60*	3.11	-13.7	3.01	-3.0	2.93	-2.8
Group Quarters	2	2	0.0	2	0.0		
Income	1969	1979	% Chg	1986	% Chg	1991	% Chg
	Census	Census	69-79	(Est.)	79-86	(Proj.)	86-91
Agg. Income($mm)	7.9	27.0	243.2	31.7	17.6	36.5	15.2
Per Capita ($)	1325	3906	194.8	4598	17.7	5308	15.4
Average Hh ($)	4775	12213	155.8	13937	14.1	15650	12.3
Median Hh ($)	4907	10014	104.1	11486	14.7	12787	11.3
Household	Income		Distribution				
	1979		1986		1991		
	Count	%	Count	%	Count	%	
Less than $ 7,500	907	40.8	807	35.2	729	31.0	
$ 7,500 - $14,999	612	27.5	636	27.8	632	26.9	
$15,000 - $24,999	438	19.7	466	20.3	494	21.0	
$25,000 - $34,999	191	8.6	241	10.5	275	11.7	
$35,000 - $49,999	65	2.9	110	4.8	162	6.9	
$50,000 - $74,999	10	0.4	28	1.2	49	2.1	
$75,000 and over	0	0.0	2	0.1	8	0.3	

*1970 Household Size Is an Estimate Based on 1970 Census Data.
Data on Income Are Expressed in "Current" Dollars for Each Respective Year.
Hh=household   Agg=aggregate

Owsley, Kentucky
County Seat: Booneville

Owsley County has no operating manufacturing plants at this time. There is no rail, air, or bus transportation into Owsley County.

There is no hospital, and only one bank. The weekly Booneville Sentinel is the only local media. The State has selected Owsley County as a primary target for economic development.

Owsley County lies about 90 miles southeast of Lexington, and 40 air miles northwest of Hazard. Although Booneville is the major community in the county and has a good variety of shopping, many residents commute to the surrounding counties for shopping, employment, and recreation. Some of the youth go as far as Lexington for a movie or a dance.

The highways in Owsley County are lined with small communities. Many of these villages have their own church, store, and gas pump. The establishment of these small communities has come in part because the terrain forces almost all housing and agricultural operations into the narrow mountain valleys through which the roads run. A few homes are found up some of the draws, but most live either in Booneville or one of the smaller communities.

The South Fork of the Kentucky River bisects the county and provides a good source of fishing both for recreation and for food supplies. Most of the land for agriculture consists of the flood plain for this river. However, this land is also the only readily available land for housing and industrial development.

Some of the land sits on coal beds. Most of the good coal deposits were mined out in the late 1970's and the mines abandoned. This has left the standard scars on the land, although some of these scars were left in better condition to regenerate vegetation and wildlife habitat. Even so, the sharply cut faces will not present a softer face until erosion takes its toll centuries down the road.

Kentucky Route 30 is the major road from Jackson to London through Booneville. Not only is it the only significant east-west route through the county, Kentucky 30 connects with Kentucky 11 just outside Booneville. Kentucky 11 is the major north-south route from Manchester to Mount Sterling. Kentucky 11 is being widened and straightened north of Beattyville. This action is expected to enable the development of a major tourism industry in the area as well as proved needed transportation relief for agricultural and industrial products.

Highways 11 and 30 run through some of the most scenic areas of the nation. The Kentucky River drainage is spectacular with waterfalls, natural arches, deep canyons with great fishing streams and dense forests.

History

Owsley County history is primarily a matter of remembering the ups and downs of timber and coal over years. The lack of flat land for agriculture and industry has kept the county small. Only in the coal-boom years of the late 1970's has there been in-migration pressure.

The rugged terrain has served to create an isolation such as has been the case in many Eastern Kentucky counties. Some cultural phenomena have developed that might seem out of place in other areas. In other areas of the country, government officials might be hard pressed to defend the hiring of their own spouses, children, and other relatives to staff their county offices. It would be termed nepotism. In Owsley County and many other Eastern Kentucky counties this is simply the way it is done.

This practice appears to be a result of the isolation felt by the county for many generations. However, with the widening of the highways, and the impact of modern communications technology, little isolation is left. A way of life is passing quickly. America's backwoods culture has all but disappeared from the scene. There are few homes in any part of the country where chickens compete with rocking chairs on the porch. Driving through Owsley County, one sees dozens of television satellite antennae. Many homes in Owsley County have a vastly greater choice of television stations than do most urban Americans.

Population

The population of Owsley County has stayed at about the 6,000 person level for several generations. Very few non-Anglo persons have ever called this county home since the first settlement by whites. With no prospects for employment at this time, it is unlikely that this pattern will change in the near future.

When the coal mines began to play out in the county in the late 1970's and early 1980's, what few Black residents there were in the county migrated out of the county in search of jobs elsewhere. It appears that these persons had no family ties to keep them in the area, and when the jobs played out, the minorities left.

Demographically there are only a few areas in which the Owsley population is any different from the rest of the state or the nation. The county is home to 101 males for every hundred females, compared to the national average of 94.5 and the state average of 95.6. The average number of persons per household is 3.02, compared with a national average of 2.75. The percentages of elderly and very young in the county are both higher than average. It appears that there are fewer than expected numbers of middle aged women.

The economy and community history may account in part for this. There are precious few jobs in the county that are of the sort that are traditionally held by women, and a woman living alone or supporting children will have a less than even chance of obtaining employment. This may also be reflected in the extremely low divorce rate and the high rate of spouse and child abuse. With 1.4 divorces per 1,000 residents compared with the national average of 5.2, some persons state that the inability of a woman to support herself and/or her family after the separation is a major determinant in whether to divorce or not.

As the economy grows, the county may see an increase in the divorce rate, a decrease in the number of persons per household, and a decrease in the men/women ration in the county. A weak county economy may limit the possibilities for personal fulfillment and family choices, and divorce with or without remarriage rates indicate the extent to which persons make family choices.

Other demographic data that appear to be linked to the economics of the county indicate that personal values within the county may be keys to the limited development of the Owsley county economy. Only about 30% of the residents have a high school education, yet 66.2 % of the total county government budget is for education compared with a national average of 44% and a state average of 53.2%.

Owsley County schools are noted for their advanced classes in computers and other technology; for their work with special children, and for the great strides in overall education over the past few years. Yet the dropout rate is well above the state average.

As in most of the counties in this study, the reported crime rate, especially for serious crimes, is significantly <u>low</u>. The national average for reported serious crimes was 5,750 in 1979. The Kentucky average was 3266, and the average in Owsley County was 576, with only 33 reported serious crimes.

Various persons in Owsley County have suggested a variety of factors reflected in this data. First, crime tends to be taken much more personally by a larger percentage of the population. Persons committing crimes tend to be known closely by their victims and their families, and family honor and family retribution become the operable systems rather than courts and jails.

Second, because the area has a rather "macho" self identity, being on the losing end of an attack of any sort, property or personal, is a blow to integrity and community standing, and an embarrassment to the victim. This appears to be close to a male equivalent of the female as rape victim. In order to defend the identity and the image, it is quite appropriate in the thinking of the county to seek retribution on a personal level, either through physical violence or through restoration of pride some other way.

Third, firearms are not purchased for crime prevention but as an everyday part of providing food for family and self. Consequently there is more respect for, and expertise in, handling weapons by the general public. The presence of these weapons in the hands of persons who use them every day might tend to deter some serious crime.

Finally, crimes that occur tend to be reported on a lower level of seriousness than the actual occurrence, indicted on a lower level yet, tried on an even lower level, and sentenced passed on a still lower level. Part of this is the result of plea bargaining, limitations on police work, and other factors throughout the country.

However, in the counties of this study it appears that the low self esteem of the victims and the professionals of the county contributes another step-down factor for numbers of reported serious crimes. Persons just seem to feel that because they themselves are not worth all that much that the crime really is not that significant. One State Trooper spoke of the embarrassment of some of the victims as they reported the crimes and noting that it was common for the victim to suggest a lower classification for a rather serious crime.

With no commercial recreational activities in the county such as movies, or bowling, and because Owsley is a dry county, the primary Saturday night activity for single men is sitting around the county court house, talking about weather, women, politics, and sports.

Perhaps violating stereotypes, however, the weather talked about is likely to be the flying weather in Europe; the women talked about are likely to be Margaret Thatcher and Indira Ghandhi; the politics discussed are the relative merits of the Contras and the Sandinistas in Nicaragua; and the sports discussion centers around the perceived greed of Major League baseball players and players' agents.

Economy

Owsley County appears to be on the edge of economic growth, and several factors seem to be supportive of the concept. First, the widening of Highways 11 and 30 will make possible for the first time real efforts to establish manufacturing and processing industries in the county. There is timber, some coal remaining, and some tobacco land in the county. There is also a hidden work force of people who would like to return to the county but cannot because there is no work. In addition the Commonwealth of Kentucky is now one of the more aggressive states in pursuit of economic development, and Owsley County is one of the primary targets in the area.

But there are also some deterring factors. The Commonwealth of Kentucky has regionalized many of their offices, and most of the contact between the residents of Owsley and the state offices must be done out of the county of residence. Regular trips for official business must be made to Jackson, Hazard, and Lexington. On these trips, there is typically time and motivation for shopping and recreation, and these activities pull money out of the county before the money has made the appropriate rounds within the county.

This regionalization has also contributed to the development of these larger cities as regional shopping centers, drawing dollars from as far as 150 miles in different directions. This process also draws much needed dollars from the poorer counties of the region. The development of Hazard as a major retail center for Eastern Kentucky has been well planned and well supported by other Kentucky officials.

Another deterrent to economic growth appears to be a previous reliance on coal for economic base support. Denise Giardina, writing in the Lexington Herald-Leader (June 28, 1987), writes eloquently of the problems with a coal-oriented economy.

"Coal companies own much land and pay almost no taxes. The local tax base is therefore too small to provide adequate services. Schools suffer, and problems with water pollution and poor roads are a further barrier to diversifying the local economy. Failure to attract new businesses allows the coal industry to maintain its stranglehold. And the vicious cycle continues."

Add to this the unemployment caused by new mining methods, union busting and the exploitation of miners in Third World countries; the turning of mine sites into armed camps with the latest in surveillance equipment; the domination of local political systems; the damage to the health and safety caused by mining conditions; and the poverty of a single-industry economy. A study of the history of mining operations all across the country reveals an industry unsurpassed for negligence, viciousness and destructiveness in the pursuit of the almighty dollar."

Coal mining in Owsley County reached its height at about 1978. However, over the next few years nearly everyone employed in the coal industry in the county had lost their jobs. Many of these persons have been able to remain in the county, although unemployed, because of the low costs of housing, extended periods of unemployment insurance, and the good cash income of a garden size plot of tobacco or marijuana.

The role of tobacco in Kentucky economy is worth noting here. As the negative role of tobacco in the world's health becomes better documented, and laws and customs move to limit the intake of tobacco products, the tobacco economy shrinks. This should obviously have a major impact on the economy of Kentucky.

However, federal crop price supports currently keep the price of harvested tobacco at an inflated level. It is this price support level that keeps the small farmer in the business of producing tobacco. That $3,000 for a garden sized plot of ground is a very welcome addition to an already stretched personal cash flow.

In addition, tobacco is a major part of the identity and self image of the region. In a county such as Owsley, with such critical self esteem problems already because of the failed coal economy and the inability to make cash money in other ways, the protection of self-image as experienced in the tobacco industry is extremely important.

When small time farmers talk about the potential loss of their tobacco cash, it is more than just a matter of money. It is the potential loss of a last-ditch effort at personal pride that is seen in some of the legislative actions. It is this threat that causes persons to make seemingly irrational statements such as "No one has really shown a link between smoking and developing cancer, and they never will."

There appears to be, however, a sense of the inevitable loss of this portion of the economy, limited as it is in Owsley county. Approximately one million pounds of tobacco is harvested annually in Owsley County. To cope with this change, it will be necessary to develop an alternative. A great gift might be, as one farmer said, to "show us something besides tobacco and marijuana we can grow on that land without losing our shirts." A farmers' cooperative with home base in Lee County serves Owsley as well.

Although Owsley County is filled with beautiful forests, good fishing streams, and decent hunting, tourism will probably not be a major industry in the near future. Most of the major scenic areas and historical sites are in neighboring counties. However, the development of these areas might have some limited spill off into Owsley. Booneville now has a small motel, Goodman's, with about a dozen rooms. The development of some bed and breakfast facilities in the area will probably occur shortly, and should be a successful and welcome addition to the county.

The options for the area appear to be limited to cottage industries, high tech production, and service work. There is some expectation that the state will develop a regional prison in the county and thus provide several hundred jobs. However, current prison thinking and political processes make this industry very akin to coal. Politically defined lengths of terms, funding for officers, political pork barrels and the need to develop internal prison industries make an economy built on prisons very unstable.

Booneville is developing as a sprawling and unorganized community within a county with only limited planning and zoning activity. Various stores and supermarkets are established in a variety of directions from downtown. One major shopping area is in an area that has been vacated by the new highway development. Another store is in an area with extremely limited and difficult parking space. Another (in an area that will probably see the most residential growth over the next decade) is caught in a small inadequate facility.

The downtown area is quite simple, with the modern county court house occupying the central portion of the town square, and small businesses on three sides around it. Some offices are located on the highways leading out of town in all directions. The downtown storefronts are all filled with a variety of businesses, from a doughnut shop to a hardware store.

The question normally rises, with all this activity in the county, why is the per capita income so low? There appear to be several possibilities. First, there is no planning or zoning, no community agreement, on the future of the community. In fact, the most talked about feature of the county is the struggle between various families and groups in the county concerning who will control and benefit from any future development. Every person interviewed in the county noted this issue.

Second, because of the inability of the community to agree on patterns of development and business practice and mutual support, the vast majority of persons go outside the county to do any serious shopping. Thus money that comes into the county through government support, welfare, coal income, or wages, is taken out of the county almost immediately and put into circulation in a neighboring county. Money that would typically roll over several times within Owsley County then rolls over several times in the neighboring counties. This seems to be especially true regarding larger lump sums of money, such as tobacco subsidies and land sales. With no major auto dealerships in the county, these sums which make good down payments go directly to neighboring counties.

Third, the community self image and the few years of successful coal industry have combined to limit the numbers of persons who otherwise would see that there is money to be made in Owsley County through a combination of hard work and training. Coal teaches that anyone can drive a coal truck or a loader, with or without a high school education. The community image teaches that any attempts to create wealth are just not going to work because "we are just plain, poor people. That's all we have ever been, and that's all we will ever be."

It seems apparent that neither statement is true, but in combination they create a certainty that any who would create wealth must go to some other area to do their work. Coal runs out, taking with it jobs for just anyone. Satellite antennas reveal high states of communications; deliveries of newspapers from various parts of the world, coupled with vacations in Europe, Central America, and Japan speak of a cosmopolitan view of the world. Discussions at Campbell's restaurant about certificates of deposit and load versus no-load funds reveal an awareness of and participation in the larger economy of the world. But potential wealth makers leave and do not return except to retire.

In the research for the county, one question seemed to bring a uniform answer. "Who does make a living here?" The nearly uniform answer was that two groups of people make it in Owsley County: Persons born in the county, and persons with some government job, from teacher to postal worker. The school system is the county's largest employer.

Medical Care and Social Services

While some programs and personnel exist in the county to care for medical and social needs, the regionalization of the care forces persons to go to Hazard or Irvine or Manchester for much of the care. A well trained and hard working ambulance crew makes medical care accessible. The public health center and the Mountain Comprehensive Health Care Corporation clinic combine to give good basic care, although limited by the lack of a county hospital and its attendant staff and equipment.

Social needs are served by a variety of agencies within the county, although regionalization again takes its toll. One major difficulty of this study has been the lack of complete records at the county level for such data as rates of alcoholism, potential suicides, food stamps, etc. The counties just do not choose to invest precious dollars in these data. The result is that planning cannot really be based on certainties of community needs and practices. The workers do the best they can with limited resources in outlining the needs of the community, but lack of data on which to build and call for funds is a significant handicap.

During the last few years a low income housing project has been developed which provides some good homes for persons in the lowest income brackets who choose to live there. These clean and modern duplexes and multiplexes provide a goodness of shelter beyond what most of the residents could provide for themselves.

Single women with families are particularly hard pressed to provide shelter in the community. However, as in many such developments, there is no provision for gardens or for recreation areas. There is no public swimming pool in the county.

The Senior Citizens' Center serves daily meals to about fifty persons and provides good opportunities for fellowship and mutual support. It also supplies opportunities for recreation, health care, and home care assistance.

Several of the persons in the housing project came into the community during the coal-boom years and have stayed behind when the boom moved on. Some are women with children who are separated or divorced from their husbands who chose to move on when the economy closed. Others have just been unable to find jobs anywhere that would provide sustenance for their families. Food stamps and commodity distribution and other support help make life bearable and enable many women in this community to devote larger blocks of time to rearing their children.

Several specific needs for added social services in the county were mentioned. There is no real counseling service in the county although several persons in a variety of positions simply try to help with their limited time and training. There is no 24-hour 'hot line' for personal assistance apart from the Sheriff's office and the fire department/ambulance service. The typical self help groups do not exist in the community. Parents Anonymous, Overeaters Anonymous, and others are not formed. There is no community food bank or emergency food supply.

The Day Care Center has been in danger of closing <u>for want of clients</u>. It seems that few women in the county can locate jobs, so stay home, taking care of the children, and resign themselves to this life. This in turn makes it less efficient to keep the center operating for those few who really need its services.

Church

Owsley County has a number of strong churches, including United Methodist, Presbyterian, Assembly of God, several Baptist groups, and others. These churches have found their respective niches in the county culture and work rather well together where appropriate.

The Presbyterian Church is a modern building along the old highway just west of town. This church is home to several of the leaders of the community. Various larger and smaller Baptist congregations are located around the county. Most of the smaller communities consist of a few homes, a store, perhaps a post office, and a small church. The denomination represented is not typically a large issue as long as the church lives.

The three United Methodist Churches are part of the Red Bird Missionary Conference. The Booneville, Warren's Chapel, and Clifty churches are all served by Waldemar Bobrowski, a missionary from Alaska who has served in the area most of his ministry.

Everyone in the county knows and respects Mr. Bobrowski for his commitment to the area and to its people. In conversations in the court house, in businesses, and on the street most persons mentioned him when asked who were the "respected leaders" of the community. Although most county-wide functions are the turf of this or that family or faction, Mr. Bobrowski seems to have good relationships with a broad range of persons in the area.

A look at the three United Methodist Churches in the county shows several things. First, the Clifty Church has a membership of 32, total expenses of $5,026, Sunday School attendance of 5, and average worship attendance of 11. The church is at approximately half the strength it was in 1973. Clifty pays $1,600 of the pastor's salary, or 6.2% of his total remuneration.

The Warren's Chapel Church has a membership of 66, total expenses of $9,986, Sunday School attendance of 38, morning worship attendance 42, and Sunday evening attendance of 32. The church pays $3,400, or 13.1% of the total pastor's remuneration. The Warren's Chapel congregation, while having one-fourth fewer members than in 1974, operates with 10 times the budget and twice the attendance as in 1974.

The Booneville congregation has a membership of 93, total expenses of $24,619, Sunday School attendance of 31, and average worship attendance of 45. Booneville supplies $13,609, or 52.5% of the pastoral support costs. The Red Bird Missionary Conference supplies another $7,323, or 28.2%. The Booneville Church is at about the same strength it was in 1974.

Second, a look at the rosters of the congregations shows that over one hundred and fifty persons from the county have positions of responsibility in the congregations. These persons represent about ninety households, or about 6% of the homes in the county. These homes are scattered about the county, giving the United Methodist Church a broad base of participants from which to continue to develop programs and services for a wide range of county needs.

Third, the churches are active now. The pastor writes in his annual report concerning the Clifty congregation, "...individual members of the church help out in the community in various ways, therefore they extend an influence in the community beyond the church's size." Then he speaks of the goals of the church...house to house visitation...10% increase in membership ...homecoming celebrations...revival services ...building fund support ...missions event...Bible study Class ...Sunday School and worship hours ...and "other activities and services".

The Warren's Chapel congregation duplicates many of these goals, and adds "begin a choir...repay Conference loan...". The Booneville church adds "increase congregational fellowship times...use assistants in worship services ...accept missional goals, i.e. hunger and Ethnic Minorities Local Church Priority."

The members of the congregations are interested in the way their faith makes an impact on the community. Although the members of the congregation are some of the strong leaders of the community, they do not see themselves that way. There is a sense that stronger leadership would do a better job of organizing the church for service as well as for impact on the economic life of the community.

The need for support and training for leadership was spoken again and again in the conversations in the community. Yet when asked what the church does for "you, as an individual and as a citizen of the community", the group responded with the same answers. "It helps me grow spiritually and mentally." "The church is my family." "The church gives me strength to cope. It's the same as if the car is running low on gas, you go to the filling station." "It teaches me to have compassion at home."

When asked what the church can provide for persons entering the business world, the group was also quite specific. "A positive attitude. Our county has been too negative, and we need to be positive."

"Encouragement to stay here and develop what potential there is here. The grass is not always greener on the other side of the fence."

"It can teach some skills, such as finances, and handling meetings, and secretarial, and budget skills to the officers." ("But we don't do much of that because we are afraid we will interfere with the pastor's role.")

What message is there, if any, for the victims of child or spouse abuse? "You don't deserve to be treated that way. You are a child of God."

What are the most exciting programs you are involved in as a congregation? "When someone goes to a national denominational meeting, we all sort of go along in spirit." "We talk and study about international needs and politics."

What are some problems you would like help with? "We spend too much time doing Conference and General Church promotions. We would like to spend the time in service rather than publicity."

General

Owsley County has a rough road ahead. Although there is a rather well developed semiskilled labor force in the county, the almost complete lack of investment funds forces any development to be of the mom and pop variety. The community self image presents a sense of impending failure for the business community, from the health spa to the hardware stores.

There is money to be made in Owsley County. It is good land for high quality purebred cattle and sheep. The people are becoming more ambitious as they begin to realize that the urban world that has been the green on the other side of the fence is not so great after all, and that what exists in Owsley County is a pretty good way of life.

County Judge Executive Dale Roberts notes "Life here is pretty good. We just haven't always seen the goodness, and because we haven't seen the goodness we have not really tried to build on it. But it's coming."

As is typical in these areas, many persons worry about the direction of impending development. In most areas, the people like their community just fine the way it is. That is, of course, except for the lack of money. In all my travels, I did not visit a community where I would be unwilling to live or to revisit.

Some direct attack on the community self-image seems to be called for in order to deal with the rather serious problems of the community. It is recognized by several persons in the community that investment money will not come into the community until the community itself begins to see itself in a better light. This may be the great task for the church, to evangelize in a way that says "We are important and worth while."

Mr. Harold Terry, a life long resident of the county and supervisor of Human Resources, was asked why he stayed in the county when he could go somewhere else, make more money, and work his way up the career ladder. He responded "I'm high on Owsley County. What can I say?"

This list of sources is provided as a sample of the types of persons interviewed in the study. All these persons were extremely helpful and supportive.
Mr. Jim Thompson, State Economic Development,
(800) 626-2930
Cindy Marcum, Store Clerk
Billy Ray Hunter, Store Owner
Marlene McIntosh, Sheriff's family
Harold Terry, Human Services Office supervisor
Dale Roberts, County Judge-Executive
The Reverend Waldemar Bobrowski, pastor
Ella Addison, Economic Insurance Office (welfare)
Donna Frost, Teacher of Gifted Children, School System
Nelson Bobrowski, Bank employee
Oneida McIntosh, housewife
Joyce Marcum, Librarian
Hickman Patrick, Bank
Eileen Price, School Librarian
Steve Addison, Special Investigator
        and others

Owsley, Kentucky   Trend Information

Population and Households

	1970	1980	%	80-86	(Proj.)	86-91	%
	Census	Census	70-80	(Est.)	80-86	(Proj.)	86-91
Population	5023	5709	13.7	5632	-1.3	5557	-1.3
Households	1460	1890	29.5	1923	1.7	1950	1.4
Household Size	3.44*	3.02	-12.2	2.93	-3.0	2.85	-2.7
Group Quarters	5	5	0.0	5	0.0		
Income	1969	1979	% Chg	1986	% Chg	1991	% Chg
	Census	Census	69-79	(Est.)	79-86	(Proj.)	86-91
Agg. Income($mm)	4.9	16.8	242.0	23.6	40.2	27.7	17.4
Per Capita ($)	979	2946	200.9	4188	42.2	4981	18.9
Average Hh ($)	3368	8967	166.2	12297	37.1	14229	15.7
Median Hh ($)	4225	6630	56.9	9692	46.2	11250	16.1
Household	Income		Distribution				
	1979		1986		1991		
	Count	%	Count	%	Count	%	
Less than $7,500	1075	56.9	785	40.8	679	34.8	
$ 7,500 - $14,999	516	27.3	604	31.4	592	30.4	
$15,000 - $24,999	210	11.1	329	17.1	391	20.1	
$25,000 - $34,999	42	2.2	121	6.3	161	8.3	
$35,000 - $49,999	35	1.9	44	2.3	74	3.8	
$50,000 - $74,999	12	0.6	32	1.7	34	1.7	
$75,000 and over	0	0.0	8	0.4	19	1.0	

*1970 Household Size Is an Estimate Based on 1970 Census Data.
Data on Income Are Expressed in "Current" Dollars for Each Respective Year.
Hh=household Agg=aggregate

McCreary, Kentucky
Major town: Whitley City

There are no incorporated cities in McCreary County. Whitley City, Stearns, and Pine Knot are "census designated places" of about 1500 persons each. McCreary County covers 427 sq. miles of the Eastern Coal Fields Region of Kentucky. The county is situated in the southern portion of the Daniel Boone National Forest.

The Cincinnati, New Orleans and Texas Pacific Railway serves Whitley City, Stearns, and Pine Knot. The county is served by U.S. 27, and Interstate 75 is 21 miles away. The Cumberland Parkway is 31 miles north of Whitley City. Six common carrier trucking companies serve the county. Knoxville, Tennessee, is the closest scheduled airline service, 107 miles away. Lexington is slightly farther away. The McCreary county airport is just northwest of Pine Knot.

Geography

As the real heart of Kentucky's Wild River Country, McCreary County is a spectacular scenic area with excellent tourism possibilities. Rocky canyons and stream beds along the Big South Fork of the Cumberland River and its tributaries present good small scale scenic wonders such as the Falls of the Cumberland and the Natural Arch. Various grades of coal underlay much of the land, with some of it being of such quality, depth, and grade to make profitable some mining in the area.

The area is heavily forested with various hardwoods and conifers. Road construction into the forested areas is comparatively easy, although cross country highway construction is more difficult because of the sharply rolling hills. As in most of Appalachia, precious little farmland is available for row crops because of the sharply breaking terrain. What little tillable land lies in the valley beds is also valuable for housing and industrial development.

Whitley City itself is a rather complete shopping area, but Oneida, Tennessee, and Somerset, Kentucky, attract many of the retail and wholesale dollars of McCreary County residents.

History

McCreary County has been a favorite of various groups of people as long as humans have lived in the area. Ancient native tribes lived along its streams, fishing, hunting, living off wild berries, roots, and leaves.

With the coming of European culture, McCreary County was a bloody frontier through most of the 18th century. Daniel Boone and Dr. Thomas Walker were two of the leaders of the European settlements through those years. Chief Doublehead was the last great chief of the Cherokee Nation, and it was he who signed the area over to the land developers of the Transylvania Company.

In the intervening years, the history of McCreary county has been one of boom and bust centering around the coal and lumber industries. Currently McCreary County is preparing something of a turnaround based primarily on hoped for tourism with the Big South Fork National River and Recreation Area. Coal mines and lumber mills in the area still operate, although at far less than capacity.

Population

Although the 1980 Census listed about 200 of the 15,634 persons in McCreary as Black, this figure seems to have decreased significantly in the last six years. Some merchants in the county could only think of some 10-15 Black persons in the county. This movement seems to be typical of the whole of Appalachia.

While many local persons speak of all those who are moving from the county, the median age within the county is 26.5 years, compared with 29.1 for the State and 30 for the nation. Several factors appear to impact this.

Although the school drop out rate is rather high, the youth remain at home participating in the family support for some time. The marriage rate is low, and the rate of births to mothers under the age of 20 is almost double the national rate. Social services and medical personnel in the area note that these births are typically to girls still living with their parents rather than married or living with a man. The average number of persons per household is 20% above the national average, and the marriage rate is only 80% of the national average.

Although McCreary County has a rather low per capita income level, and some of the homes in the county are apparently residences of persons with very little money, the homes, businesses, streets, and recreation facilities reflect a strong pride in the community. Yards are neat and clean, well mowed and landscaped. Even the tiniest of homes that might be on an economic par with low-income housing in urban areas, seem well- kept. This might reflect the 74% rate of owner occupied housing in the county, compared with the national 64% rate.

It might also reflect the manner in which many of the homes are obtained. Frequently, parents will sub-divide their property to give a son or daughter title to enough land for a house and lawn and garden. The young people then build a minimum home, paying for it as they go, and expecting to add to the home as a family comes along. In this area, homes of 600 to 800 square feet are commonly built along these lines, and young persons find themselves with a permanent residence, a close multigenerational extended family, and very little housing debt. With this arrangement, even very low wages can provide sophisticated television and entertainment centers, quality automobiles, and frequent national and international travels.

This arrangement also makes extended periods of unemployment such as are common in the lumber and coal industries much more tolerable. If things get terribly bad, GMAC takes back the four wheel drive pickup, CityCorp gets the television and stereo, and the bank gets the sofa. With replacements from second hand stores and neighbors or family, burning wood and coal for heat, and keeping a good garden, extended periods of unemployment can be tolerated, though rarely enjoyed.

Economy

McCreary County has been a producer of high grade low sulphur coal for several centuries. The total coal supply is not in immediate danger of running out, but the coal is becoming more costly and difficult to mine. At times almost all available workers were engaged in coal production, and at other times very few were employed.

Lumber has been another historic product of the county, with the railroads busy shipping either coal or lumber to eastern and northern cities. However, the lumber market is now largely a production tool for regional furniture centers and for local building needs.

Service industries and government have replaced mining and lumber as the primary employers of the county. The school system is the largest single employer in the county. Because the county is currently in an economic slump, county and state government employees are limited in number. The Federal Government is represented by a small but growing number of persons in mine supervision, forestry, highways, and the rapidly developing Big South Fork National River and Recreation Area.

Although the county currently lists four motels and over twenty restaurants, it is clear that more tourist industry will develop in the area over the next dozen years. Additional facilities will be constructed and persons trained and hired to cope with the estimated one million persons per year who will come to the River and Recreation Area. Currently just over one hundred and fifty thousand come for this resource, and the facilities are beginning to find their limits.

Although the future looks rosy to the State and to other outside experts in the field of tourism, few persons in the county see things that way. There is a sense of pessimism, or "show me", about the great predictions. There is also an unwillingness to invest sums of money and energy in projects that do not fit the community identity and life style. Tourism is not seen as a typical way of life in the area.

The development of a service oriented commercial sector has not met with strong negative feelings, but with a doubtful passivity on the part of most merchants. Catering to the whims of the rather specialized tourists who might come to the area does not complement the self identity of the residents of this Appalachian `macho' community. The greatest task of the developers of the Recreation Area may be the restructuring of the community identity and purpose to make the industry possible. It may not be easy for families and institutions to maintain their close integrity as the community fills with short term visitors.

Another economic issue alluded to above is the physical redevelopment of the towns of Whitley City, Pine Knot, and Stearns. These towns straddle the once busy but now nearly ignored `Old US 27'. The major shopping centers, motels, restaurants, clinics, and other commercial operations now extend along the new highway, creating a strip city approximately ten miles in length and taking most of the business from the old areas, just a few hundred yards away.

There is a good retail district along the new highway which includes a number of quite respectable shopping centers. These have good potential for volume and for variety. However, many persons drive thirty miles to Somerset to the large stores there.

The reasons given by those who drive the distance typically center around the inability to purchase certain items or services in McCreary County, the attractiveness of the County shopping areas (or lack of attractiveness), and a new found identity as a cosmopolitan shopper. Items and services apparently unavailable in the county include new automobiles, computer technology, hospitals and their attendant medical specialists, and passive recreation (movies, plays, etc.).

The impact of shopping outside the county for merchandise found in the county is that money which comes into the county and would typically be `rolled over' four or five times within the county before leaving in various forms is rolled over only once or twice. A dollar net into the county economy becomes only two dollars rather than four or five dollars in the economy.

The merchants who opposed the opening of the Wal Mart store in the area were thus faced with a real dilemma. They could compete with a large modern superstore in their midst that would help the overall local economy but perhaps hurt their own business, or force the store to stay some thirty miles away, knowing that it would hurt both their businesses and the county economy as a whole. Wal Mart settled in Somerset.

Church

McCreary County pays much attention to its churches. There is no question that church life is a large part of the personal and corporate identity of the people of the area, whether they participate in the church or not.

Many persons see the Church as an extension of the family and, in some cases, the business or elected office. Some see the church as interested only in saving souls from Hell. But no one I spoke with in the County saw the whole of Christ's Church as being unimportant to the everyday life of the people in the county.

The individual churches of the county have their corporate identities, but the churches who participate in the very active Ministerial Association seem to be both the best know and most respected. These churches are the founders and supporters of the Christian Care Center in Whitley City.

This ministry provides medical care, social and psychological services, and a common identity of caring and supporting for the people of the county. The Board of Directors is primarily made up of the pastors who participate in the Ministerial Association.

Working closely with the McCreary County Health Center, and the private physicians of the County, the Care Center is part of an above-average health care provider network. Although there is no hospital in the County, access to Lake Cumberland Medical Center at Somerset is relatively easy and quick.

The churches are known to be a significant part of this team. In addition, a primary summer activity for all ages is church league softball, played at the county park. Many persons in the county find good value in regular attendance at the many revivals occurring throughout the summer in the various churches. Spiritual life is not neglected.

The impact of the church on the economic life the community is difficult to measure, but not difficult to notice. Bringing medical and social services to the central county eliminates the need for numbers of persons to go outside the county for services, and thus for shopping. Providing a variety of educational and spiritual and social programs has to bring the community together in cooperation, mutual support, and social identity.

As the churches attempt to cope with the major problems of the community, including spouse abuse, child abuse, and drug problems, the church is brought also to face the issues of financial limitations and institutional distrust. While the divorce level is low, social workers and pastors speak of the many persons who contemplate divorce but do not follow through. The evidence is that those who are most likely to be victimized in spouse abuse are also persons who feel themselves either incapable or unworthy of supporting themselves (and perhaps the children) if the divorce is finalized, so the divorce is not completed.

The United Methodist Churches of the county are small and do not easily support themselves. The congregations speak of themselves as being small and insignificant. However, several persons in the county, both in and out of the church, spoke of the encouragement and support various persons of the congregations gave those who were searching for a better way of life. The Whitley City congregation was noted for its acceptance of persons who were struggling with personal identity and worth, including those with spouse abuse problems.

None of the three congregations, Whitley City, Pleasant Run, and Mill Creek, operates with a specified budget. The Whitley City congregation had an income of about $29,000 in 1986. The pastor, Charles Spice, receives a $3,700 salary supplement from the Annual Conference. The pastor of the Pleasant Run charge, Darren Godby, who is now finishing high school, receives very small compensation.

The attendance at Whitley City is about 70, and Pleasant Run and Mill Creek have about 20 each. The Roman Catholic congregation attendance is about 50; Church of God 100; the 30 or so Baptist congregations together number about 600 in attendance. Other congregations in the county are smaller. The three United Methodist congregations consistently pay 100% of their apportionments.

The Whitley City Administrative Council meets two or three times per year, mostly to consider building maintenance and festivals such as the Easter and Christmas programs. At Christmas the congregation presents a musical, and at Easter the congregation participates in the community Sunrise Service. Vacation Bible School welcomes about 40 children. The United Methodist Women meets monthly, with a continuing project of quilting for the orphanage at Versailles.

The Whitley City congregation has experienced some good growth over the past five years. The congregation is convinced that this has resulted from three factors:
(1) The continuing service and evangelistic personal outreach on the part of the pastor and the members;
(2) The Sunday morning 30-minute radio broadcast on the local station; and
(3) The participation of the congregation in the work of the Christian Care Center. The work at the Care Center includes participation in the G.E.D. program, volunteer driving of disabled persons, and receptionist work.

General Comments

McCreary County should see some economic growth over the next dozen years as both tourism and retail industries stabilize. If fuel costs go up, that would limit tourism, perhaps, but be a help to the retail stores in the county. If fuel costs go down, that should help tourism but hurt the retail industry. The widening of US 27 will bring more tourists to town, but take more shoppers to Somerset and Oneida.

Retail and service establishments in the county will need to learn to compete with the markets in Somerset and Oneida. Beautification of shopping areas, modernization of facilities, training of workers to treat shoppers as honored guests, and the extension of varieties to make county shopping possibilities more complete will all help in the process.

McCreary County offers a unique opportunity right now for small businesses to start. With over 15,000 persons in the relatively compact county, and most of them clustered around Whitley City, conditions are ripe for small business establishment. The State of Kentucky is pursuing development of the county quite aggressively.

McCreary, Kentucky   Trend Information

Population and Households

	1970	1980	% Chg	1986	% Chg	1991	% Chg	
	Census	Census	70-80	(Est.)	80-86	(Proj.)	86-91	
Population	12548	15634	24.6	16409	5.0	17026	3.8	
Households	3503	4853	38.5	5258	8.3	5612	6.7	
Household Size	3.51*	3.16	-9.9	3.06	-3.0	2.98	-2.7	
Group Quarters	298	298	0.0	298	0.0			
Income	1969	1979	% Chg	1986	% Chg	1991	% Chg	
	Census	Census	69-79	(Est.)	79-86	(Proj.)	86-91	
Agg. Income ($mm)	14.3	50.7	256.0	74.5	46.7	91.4	22.7	
Per Capita ($)	1136	3246	185.7	4538	39.8	5367	18.3	
Average Hh ($)	4030	10394	157.9	14092	35.6	16219	15.1	
Median Hh ($)	4382	7553	72.4	11038	46.1	12600	14.2	
Household	Income		Distribution					
	1979		1986		1991			
	Count	%	Count	%	Count	%		
Less than $ 7,500	2420	49.9	1910	36.3	1750	31.2		
$ 7,500 - $14,999	1344	27.7	1524	29.0	1553	27.7		
$15,000 - $24,999	772	15.9	1017	19.3	1169	20.8		
$25,000 - $34,999	196	4.0	493	9.4	612	10.9		
$35,000 - $49,999	63	1.3	200	3.8	347	6.2		
$50,000 - $74,999	47	1.0	65	1.2	109	1.9		
$75,000 and over	11	0.2	49	0.9	72	1.3		

*1970 Household Size Is an Estimate Based on 1970 Census Data.
Data on Income Are Expressed in "Current" Dollars for Each Respective Year.
Hh=household Agg=aggregate

The Mystery

What is so different about these counties that keeps them at the poverty level year after year?

The following list of subjects appears to be areas in which this group of counties, as a whole, varies widely from state or national trends. It would not be wise for the researcher to make personal evaluations of the rightness or wrongness of these trends. Rather, we have made the attempt to discover the reasons wherever possible. The personal interviews we conducted attempted to focus on these issues. Our attempt was to only learn the reasons for these departures and their impact on the population.

Typically, it was only necessary to mention the area of discussion to get a lot of community response. The persons we interviewed were quite literate as to these details as a general rule, and were eager to share their thoughts. It was obvious in every county that the population was well aware of their standing.

1. Per capita income in these counties was the lowest in the nation in 1986, ranging from a low of barely $3,000 to a high of nearly $6,000. By comparison, many counties in the US average over $15,000.

2. Population growth in these counties averages over 1% per year. Some have growth rates as high as 7.3%/year. Some are losing population at the rate of nearly 2% per year as persons leave for jobs or die early of a lack of medical care.

3. The males to females ratio in these counties is 100.1, or 6% higher than the national average. The range is 89-119.

4. The median age within these counties is 25. The national median age is 30. The county range is 19.2-33.

5. In these counties, 21.78% of births are to unmarried women, and in the nation, 15.6. The Range is 5-33.

6. The Birth rate in these counties is 24.34 per 100,000 persons, compared to 15.9 in the nation. The range is 5-37.

7. The marriage rate in the counties is 7.04 per 100,000 persons, compared with 10.6 in the nation. At the same time, the divorce rate is 2.4, compared with 5.2 per 100,000 in the nation.

8. Health care seems to be a major problem. Some ratios (per 100,000 persons) are:

	Counties	Nation	Range
Physicians	26.83	173.7	0-110.5
Dentists	17.79	51.7	0-47.84
Reg. Nurses	141.78	453.8	0-382
Hosp. Beds	246	611	0-884

9. Most counties with recorded data for crime record significantly lower crime rates than the national average. In some counties there is an almost total lack of reported crime. Of course, Native American reservation crime is unreported in these statistics.

10. An average of 49% of housing units lack complete plumbing facilities for exclusive use of the residents.

11. There are 93 jobs for every 100 persons in the work force in these counties. Yet in some of the counties, persons come in from neighboring counties in large numbers to work. Typically, these "invaders" from other areas come for government or industrial jobs.

    Additionally, the number of jobs available in a county counts a part time job as one. Families with two parents in the household will be considered as holding one job within the home. Then if either of the parents works outside the home, that is another job.

    If the family operates a farm, no matter how small, that is considered another job. A family of two, living on a small farm, with both adults working part time jobs away from the place of residence as well, is counted as holding four jobs in this data. This appears to be an obvious failure of the data reporting system in place.

12. On March 1, 1979, the unemployment rate in the counties was 15.77, more than double that of their respective states and comparing with 10% nationally. The range was 1.7-33.

13. 12.5% of the female work force was unemployed, compared with a national average of 7%. The range was 1-23.

14. The 1981 per capita income of the counties was $5531, compared with $10,495 nationally. The range in 1981 for these counties was $3122-$9868.

15. The farmland in these counties has very low value. In 1978, the value of the farmland in the counties averaged $296 per acre compared with $628 nationally. The range is $86-$863. The family farms are quite large in most areas, and a large portion of the income is from livestock operations except in the Black counties.

16. While the exact ratios are as yet unclear because of inadequate data gathering by the federal government, it is certain that these counties have a higher portion of undefined causes of death than do their neighboring counties. This may reflect low health maintenance resources.

17. In these counties, nearly one third of the total residents of the county are involved in a move into or out of the county each year. The average county in this study shows a net loss of 296 persons from migration. Yet some counties show a net gain. Ethnic patterns for migration are not at all clear.

18. The total of transfer payments, representing the most accurate measure of total unearned income to the population of the county (sometimes called various forms of welfare but actually a sense of total outside support including agricultural subsidies, etc.) is lower than the national or respective state averages is $1239, compared with a national average of $1485. The range is $763.36 to $1808.08.

19.   A concept that is difficult to measure is the relationship of individuals with various institutions such as marriage and family living. There seems to be a very high percentage of persons simply living together without benefit of formal marriage. One question raised is whether this results in added poverty or results from it. It may be both, it may be neither, but it certainly appears to be some factor in the community mix.

     It is also hard to note the relationships with agencies such as churches, governmental offices and social programs. It seems that neither community based volunteer social institutions nor the various agencies are of any strength in these counties. There is a low rate of marriage, crime reported to police and voter registration and participation.

Puzzling...

     There must be answers. It is not enough just to recognize the economic poverty of these counties. There must be answers as to why the income is so low.

     Most of the data in this report is found in the 1983 or later City and County Data Book. Some additional data is from other Bureau of the Census publications, and from state and Federal personnel with economic responsibilities in these areas.

Question: In 1980 there were 3136 counties in the United States. Of the counties listed in this study, seven are listed in Row 133 as having ranking below 3100. At least one is ranked as high as 1829 in median PCI in 1979. One of these counties saw an increase of $1,405 in PCI, and another has seen a decrease of $1,008.

     What has created changes in PCI in these areas to such extent as this? What local or wider events have shaped the relative placements of counties rankings of PCI data?

Answer: Having visited these counties, it has become clear to me that two or three factors have made particularly great differences in them.

     First, some of the states have begun again to work with the local counties to improve their economic situation. Of particular interest are the existence of grants and low interest loans, great publicity, and business and planning training and support.

     Second, Some areas have been particularly either hit hard or given great relief by environmental factors such as weather and hazardous materials disposal.

     Third, technology has led the way to massive changes in local industry, either positive or negative. The fresh pea industry of Conejos County was wiped out by a changing technology. The same could be said for the spinach industry of Zavala County.

Question: In most of the counties of this study, there was at least one person making $50,000+ in 1979. Who are these people, and what do they do that gives them such financial strength in some of the poorest of counties?

Answer: There is usually one or two persons or corporate families making this kind of money in each county, except in the northern Native American counties. They have found ways to control the massive acreage and/or human labor to produce their profit. Often they are able to do this with the support of federal subsidies or grants. Occasionally a commercial franchise produces these profits. The only two consistent financially strong institutions in the environment of these counties are the federal government and Wal-Mart.

     Additionally, a number of physicians and attorneys have been able to position themselves into wealth. This is often done through tax supported funding.

     Nearly all other persons in this bracket are direct government employees such as postal employees or contractors, Bureau of Indian Affairs supervisors or physicians, or Interstate Highway supervisors.

Question: The counties with the greatest poverty in the USA over a long period of time may well be Starr, Maverick, and Zavala in Texas and Mora in New Mexico. These are the only counties in the current study listed in a 1970 list of fifteen counties with the highest percentage of persons below the poverty level.

On this list, these counties are ranked this way:

#1 Starr, Texas

#4 Maverick, Texas

#5 Zavala, Texas

#6 Mora, New Mexico

In 1979, the poverty level range was $3,686 to $14,812.

What has happened in Mora County, New Mexico, and Zavala County, Texas, that have moved these counties nearly off the current list while Starr and Maverick have stayed approximately even? Why have Starr and Maverick counties remained near the head of the poverty list?

Answer: Zavala County is moving up the list primarily because the efforts of La Raza have begun to pay off in some rather strange ways. Although La Raza brought in quite a bit of federal and private money during its peak, that was only a drop in the bucket as far as real income is concerned.

However, much of it was apparently put to good use in developing an infrastructure of public housing, utilities, buildings and roads within Crystal City itself. When the rest of the community finally decided to work together, at least partly as resistance to La Raza, there was a substantial material community resource with which to work. Now, although La Raza is pretty much a thing of the past, it has left a legacy of material goods that is very important to the self image of the community.

Mora County, on the other hand, is beginning to come around only because it is about half way between the city of Las Vegas, New Mexico, and a couple very important snow ski resorts. Several dozen persons from Mora County make the fifty mile drive to the resorts for employment. The pay is not great, but it is better than anything available in Mora County.

Mora is also beginning to see some results from its tree farming, its retirement possibilities for persons with modest income, and some traffic flow to Taos and the ski areas.

Question: Why have the South Dakota counties become the "core" of the current list?

Answer: The primary factor, of course, is current and past racism. Unlike the Black Americans in the south, the Native Americans have historically never been valuable, particularly as slaves as the Black Americans were (and therefore welcome) in mainstream U.S. Anglo culture. They have also resisted the concept of moving into the Anglo culture.

Given these two feelings, when the Native Americans have been given land for apartheid (oops, scratch that) reservations, they did not powerfully rebel when forced upon the harshest lands of the continent. The resulting destruction of self esteem has not yet been healed. In fact, many now see is a mark of pride that the Native Americans are even able to survive this long. Some are even beginning to turn their fortunes around.

It must be noted, however, that South Dakota as a state is no more racist than any other. The state is giving some assistance (although not a lot, partly because it does not have much to give in the Reagan years) to the tribes as they face the issues of poverty and hunger. The problem has been with the levels of the federal and state bureaucracies and administrations that really do not have to deal face to face with dissatisfied persons (voters).

Question: In the 1980 ranking of counties of the U.S.A. with the highest percentage of Black residents, counties with rankings include:

#2   Jefferson, Mississippi

#7   Tunica, Mississippi

#63 Lee, Arkansas

Can the persistent presence of these counties and a large number of other southern Black counties on the poverty rolls be attributed to anything but racism?

Answer: The only other particularly relevant matter is the changing technology of farm labor, particularly in the cotton industry. What used to require two or three thousand workers now requires fifteen or twenty. Those excess workers are still in town, unemployed, waiting for opportunity in their homeland.

Question: Crime statistics are very unclear. In some areas crime appears to be very low. In most of the counties which include Reservations, complete crime data has not been available to me yet. Most of the crime on reservations is handled by Tribal Police, and is not reported as part of the Uniform Crime Statistics Report. Additionally, record keeping on reservations seems to be inordinately poor. Why?

Answer: Even in those counties with no reservations, crime rates seem exceedingly low. This may be a function of the minimum amounts of funding for local law enforcement under the current political structures. In that case many crimes simply go unreported because victims and witnesses do not assume an ability of law enforcement agencies to do anything about crime or any other social problem.

This attitude may also have something to do with the extremely low rates of marriage, divorce, Supplemental Security Income payments, and transfer payments. This issue may be the largest single issue of concern for the Church in action in these areas.

At least two of the counties, Elliott and Owsley in Kentucky, have the reputation locally of having almost no one drafted or volunteer to serve in the military during World Wars I and II. If this is accurate, it may reflect a very limited interest in participating in the social and political institutions. In this case, the evangelism of the Church, political parties and all manner of social issues organizations might be as important as any action in rekindling such interest.

The Totality of Poverty

One of the peculiarities of being human is that, like it or not, one's dollars do have a direct bearing on every facet of human existence. Money may not buy happiness, but having it or not having it certainly has an impact on ones happiness or depression, bitterness or joy. It shapes the culture of the community. It is the driving force behind health matters. It profoundly forms the basis of educational processes. It targets every sense of the Bill of Rights, from Freedom of the Press to Freedom of Religion.

In the study we found very happy and satisfied persons in every county. Yet even these people, to a person, always were able to note, even with a smile on their face, that life would be a little better if only.....

On the other hand, only a few people were able to come up with any concrete plan to improve their own situation. Talking with them, I discovered that almost all of them had been able to dream some dream of improvement at some time in the past, only to see those dreams shattered by the reality of their own inabilities or the grinding poverty of the community.

The most bitterness was directed at the major institutions of life (federal and state governments, large banks, even charitable agencies such as the Red Cross and the Church). These institutions had made big splashes of promises to assist dreams to come true. Then when the plan was put to paper and ready to implement, the carpet was pulled from under the dreamer by the institution.

The two chief institutions suffering the verbal blows of these people were the federal government (particularly the Reagan administration) and the Church. The reasons for this blaming were easy to be seen in almost every county. Unfulfilled promises, hoarded resources, outlandish personal salaries for bigwigs and cutting benefits to the local community in the name of cutting costs elsewhere are seen in every poverty stricken area of the nation.

The Church and government are just two of the culprits, but perhaps the most visible. Perhaps this is because these two make the highest promises and end up delivering the least value of all institutions. At least that is the view of most of the participants in the study.

Without doubt the most frustration is vented toward the federal government. The frustration voiced is not frequently a matter of calling for more "social welfare" programs or money.

Rather, the words talk about the people having been at one time in a better position with good hopes for the future. Then the government, for political reasons, changes its policies and the channels of its influence, and the dreams of the community are shot down.

There is an old saying that when somebody wins, somebody else has to lose. The trouble is that with the limited resources or the isolation or the culture of these counties, they tend to lose at every governmental or other bureaucratic turn. At least they have lost often enough in the past that there is little or no hope in any future turns of the government to give a better life here.

Culture

None of the cultures in the study encourage their population to make a choice to be poor. Even during the study I have heard persons from both within and without the counties say about someone else, "They just want to be poor." That is not true of any person I discovered in the study. What is true is that all cultures in this study have found ways to assist persons to cope with low cash income. Some even accept it to the point of comfort.

Coping with low cash income can mean a variety of things. In some cultures, the development of a macho image of operating with little or no cash carries on even when times are better and there is money around. Even the pipefitters of Kentucky, some of the highest paid blue collar workers of America, see themselves as "poor but proud".

In almost all cultures cashless modes of commerce take shape. Goods and services are bartered according to perceived value rather than by stated cash value. The particular items of trade that do bring in cash or are most valued in bartered take on a sort of religious significance. In eastern Kentucky that item is tobacco.

For whatever reason, the "good old days" are not remembered. I was quite surprised at this. Every county I entered had at one time or another in the last thirty years been in some sort of boom. Instead of remembering or attempting to replicate that, it was pushed into the background. Often it was only as I was leaving a county that someone would admit, "Well, it hasn't always been this way here. Back in 1978.......".

The role of women in all these counties appears to be quite limited yet expanding steadily. Some of the strongest and steadiest workers I met were women who were filling jobs at mid-level management positions, mostly in government. The ethnicity of the women holding these relatively secure jobs seemed to make little difference in the counties.

In every county I found at least one person, in their middle to late thirties, a throwback to the "love" culture of the 60's, who is working hard to make their county a better place. Some of these are in agriculture, others in government, some in the Church. None that I found were in commercial activity. All of them are in positions where they do not expect to profit financially, but the people around them will if these `servants' are encouraged to keep working.

Occasionally cultures clash in ways that may lead not only to low per capita income but to real poverty. The most notable case of this I saw was with the Navajo people and their clash with Anglo land agents. To the Anglo, land is non- personal. To the Navajo, land has divine character, a beloved part of life.

The Navajo doesn't dicker. To the Navajo, by tradition and culture it is an insult to bargain. When a price is named, that is the price.

When the land agent comes to buy the land for railroad or highway, even in good faith, the Navajo hears that there is no choice, and gives up claim to land even for a pittance. It is not just the land that is now gone, it is part of eternity, of heaven. God has been betrayed, and the Navajo could do nothing about it. That is a poverty of heart.

There seem to be four closely related community personality characteristics for these counties that impact economic development: low self esteem, inability to work cooperatively, inability to relieve tension, and impatience.

In the instance just cited, these seem to control the situation. The Navajo learns to see one's self in a lesser light after having been through the situation a time or two. The truth that higher levels of self esteem are important to increased productivity and economic growth has been demonstrated over and over again since the middle ages.

Every so-called advanced society in the world is judged to be that on the basis of its own self esteem. Henry Ford realized that the automobile would become a world force only if enough people saw themselves as wealthy enough (and therefore good enough, worthy enough,) to be possessors and controllers of this fine piece of machinery.

He began to pay his workers enough that they could actually afford to purchase the automobile for themselves, and a world-wide revolution in self esteem was born. Yet today many persons in the world cannot afford an automobile or even a television set. It is these people that society says are "backward" or "poor". Even persons who deliberately choose not to own the landmarks of an advanced culture are classified as "poor".

Imagine the impact of 200 years of this on the people. The Navajo is taught not to bargain or dicker, or to "trade cooperatively for the best interests of all." Pretty soon the Navajo simply sees the Navajo as being unworthy or incapable of fighting back when any important matter is on the line. Years of this sense of low self esteem are the necessary foundations of both slavery and the ethnic rip off.

Cooperative work in an industrialized society assumes a stance of open discussion back and forth of the value or lack of value of a particular effort, task, or product. It is not necessarily true that this value be in terms of financial arrangements. The value may be in matters of the presence of the supernatural spirits, or in marital arrangements, or in any other matter which either of the would-be cooperators find to be of personal or corporate value. It is this discussion of the relative merits that must institute cooperative trade and effort.

The Navajo is caught in a bind that the culture cannot alleviate as the land is now gone, desecrated by those who ignore its spiritual life. They see themselves as somehow not worth as much in simple human terms as those who live in square houses, drive big cars, watch television, and control the ancient lands of the Navajo people.

This creates an enormous tension in the Navajo family, the community, and the Navajo Nation. Many of the efforts within the Navajo Nation to stabilize the community and bring economic growth to the area are destroyed by this tension within the hearts of the people.

When the Navajo communities do realize that poverty is not necessary and that they need not see themselves as being worthless as compared with those who have raped their land and their communities, the attempt at turnaround becomes almost a panic situation. As in most revolutions, the first and worst destruction is done to their own institutions and homes and organizations because that is the only place they feel a power to change things.

"Right now!" "They have been in office for six months and still there are no new jobs!" This impatience which is necessary for change, but is also the breedings ground of violent revolution, is one of the deadliest enemies of structured economic growth. Rash decisions tend to be made that turn more of the resources of the nation over to the ever more despised and hated Anglo capitalists and politicians.

In the process, of course, the Navajo People (as do all populations that speak a general tongue other than that of the majority population) lose a lot of headway simply in the difficulties of language translation. This is the case even in some of the professions as attorneys, physicians and clergy develop languages hidded from the common person.

Many Native Peoples across the nation did not object to strenuously when the railroads were being built across the continent. After all, there is a lot of land, and these tracks are only a long step apart. A few buildings here and there, even some small towns along the way, could not be difficult to live with.

What the peoples were probably told, but did not comprehend because of the language and cultural differences, was that the railroad capitalists were being given ownership and control of the land 100 miles to either side of the tracks. This constituted, in many cases, a complete theft of the land peopled by the Natives by the railroad capitalists.

This may seem to be an over-simplification, of course, but according to The Reverend Fred Yazzi, quite accurate.

These community traits are generally recognizes as being the responsibility of the Church. Yet when I asked what value the church has in the community in its work of economic development, the consensus was "none'.

Resources

All fourteen counties I visited have at least some resources that might be capitalized for economic development. In some cases the resource is limited to a likely location for a retirement community. In other cases tourism is a possibility. Everywhere there is some possibility. Some areas have good prospects for a revival of agriculture or of new manufacturing.

It appears that the chief reason for the lack of development in these areas can be traced to an inability to work cooperatively. In many areas states are taking on the role of facilitator for resource development. In all areas I have visited, economic development is understood to be a task of the state. In some areas the state is accused of ignoring the needs of small isolated communities.

Every resource has its up and down periods. In every case of this study, a number of resources in each of these fourteen counties have been in down cycles in the same calendar year, 1986. Some cycles last longer than others. As technology changes, many of these cycles are shortened dramatically. The up cycle of gold mining in San Juan County, Utah lasted nearly three hundred years. That same amount of gold could be taken from the county now in about five years. Counting the people who design and build and finance the machinery, it would probably take more people now to do the job.

When the last resource available (government) pulls the plug in the same year that other resources are slumping, the county really has a bad year. Zavala County, Texas is an example of this disharmonic cycling of resources. Cotton was looking bad, but melons were doing well, the spinach and okra markets were up. Then the La Raza Unida movement began, and pulled in huge financial resources from the federal and state governments. People flocked to Zavala County.

Then all the markets went sour because of technology and climate. The federal government administration changed, drying up many of the resource programs. The state went into a tailspin because of prices of oil, wheat, and cattle. The state found it could not resource the county as it had previously done. The county, which had not had to work cooperatively for at least three decades, could not cope with sudden loss of 90% of its financial strength.

In most counties there is enough diversity of industries to cover some bad years, but in the counties of this study the diversity just happened to bring the various resources into slump cycles at the same time. Contributory factors such as international politics and technology seem to be out of the control of local hands, and low self esteem is exacerbated.

Community

Community tensions, as often as not, arise from a misdirected blame for economic woes. Probably 90% of the people I interviewed in this study blamed some specific other person or group in the community for the economic woes of the area. Most of the time it appeared to me that the blame could at least be spread a lot farther.

In only one of the counties (Owsley, Kentucky) was there consensus among those interviewed as to which specific individuals were responsible for the low economic state. In this county every person interviewed could name these individuals and describe their impact on the county economy. As I looked closer I am convinced that their real impact is the result of the system of government with which they work and is an accepted part of the community identity.

In other words, the community has chosen this particular form of government which negates cooperation and upward mobility, and places the blame for the systemic failure on the individuals who run it. The community also continues to re-elect them.

The inability to overcome these tensions and establish a consistent pattern of cooperation not only limits the efficiency of economic development work, but it also acts as a red flag to any outside industries considering relocating into the area. Few businesses choose to locate in an area of community turmoil.

One consistent pattern that has caught my attention is the location of Wal Mart Stores. In at least one county next to the counties I have visited there is a Wal Mart Store. In every case a significant portion (sometimes over half) of the income of that Wal Mart Store is derived from sales to residents of the study county.

It appears that lack of community pride and commitment is as much behind this drive to shop elsewhere as is any motive. There is a consensus across the counties that, if it is available in this county it is not really as good as it is in the next county.

I did quick informal surveys in several counties concerning relative prices. With the exception of loss leader items or some specific bulk-wholesale items, prices in the poorest counties themselves averaged less than 2% higher than in their neighboring counties.

The practice of purchasing outside the county is very expensive to the county. In Conejos County, Colorado, each shopping trip to Alamosa is estimated to cost the county $70. This represents lost revenues, recycled dollars, gasoline dollars that could have purchased goods or services in Conejos or been invested or placed in savings, and other losses. The dollars are not recycled through local businesses but through businesses in Alamosa who do not recycle their expenses and profits through Conejos County businesses. One still has to purchase groceries. In other words, a single shopping trip to Alamosa for $30 of groceries actually costs over $100. Not much is saved at that rate.

In every county some one or some group is attempting to put something together. The people in these counties are not lazy. They work hard to get ahead. There is no evidence to support any statement that these persons are poor because they choose to be. They may, however, have made choices that have not paid off. That is a risk we all take.

Many people in the counties believe that if they were to attempt to establish a business, they would fail, so they do not try. Many sincerely believe they are not important enough in the eyes of God to get any support there! The Protestant Work Ethic relied on an understanding that it is important to the relationship with God for one to work as hard as possible, and that God would reward the worker. In these counties people work hard but without that sense of reward by God.

Others, however, are people who are capable of creating wealth for themselves and others, are doing their best, and need the support of the community and the Church. In every county where there is a United Methodist Church some leader in the congregation is recognized as a leader in the economic development of the community. In two counties, Zavala, Texas and Owsley, Kentucky, the pastor was recognized as in that select group. In Zavala County, both pastors were in that group.

There seem to be two distinct ways of creating wealth in our system. One of these is to create wealth for one's self by taking from others. That is clearly not acceptable. The other method is creating wealth by first creating wealth for others and then sharing in their wealth. That seems to be appropriate. Accurate or not, this is the image that surrounds Lee Iacocca. Few people in America resent his millions for he is credited with making a lot of other people wealthy first.

Regionalization of services has done great damage to the economic development of some of the counties in the study. In most of the counties of the study it is impossible to register for any federal program within the county outside of some agricultural programs such as weed control and erosion control. The development of regional hospitals, clinics, colleges, and other services makes some kind of financial sense, but it spells the death of many small outlying communities.

This regionalization of services forces persons to leave their own counties and local businesses to go to larger areas. While there they "just do a little shopping". This also strips the outlying communities of needed leadership and community identity and purpose. Kentucky has probably done this more intentionally than any other state.

There is a strong distrust of all institutions in these counties. Social clubs, colleges, governments, churches and businesses only have value as they happen to be able to deliver a direct service in the community. The stabilizing effect on the community of long-term institutional life has little or no value.

Little thought is given to any time period beyond the next few days in any of these counties except among the Native Americans. Many, even among those with the least, look ahead not to life after death but to later years in this life when things will be better. The kind of planning that would make possibility the development of additional hospitals, schools, industries and other community anchors seems to be lacking in almost every area.

Health

The health issues that have arisen from the study have pointed us in some surprising directions. The factors that have added most to the weakness in health care have come as much from bureaucracies that have sprung up as means to assist in the development of health care, medical practitioner greed and a search for community identity as from inability to pay for medical care.

In some of these counties, medical care within the county is simply nonexistent. In most cases, any medical care must be sought in neighboring counties. In some cases, notably Kentucky, the regionalization of medical and educational facilities has been carried out knowing full well the devastating impact on the local citizens.

Many Kentucky counties, some of the poorest in the land, have had even minimal medical care stripped away by the move to regionalize medical care. This regionalization has benefitted some persons.

First, physicians and administrators of these major medical centers have been able to raise their income to truly exorbitant levels. Medical specialists, particularly, have been able to further specialize at little or no financial risk.

Second, politicians have been able to point to these great facilities with pride during their re-election campaigns. They simply do not get the idea that a smaller and smaller percentage of citizens can actually take advantage of the regionalized facilities and services.

Third, medical industry ancillary services, ranging from hotels and motels to cleaning services to medical equipment suppliers, have been able to develop virtual monopolies over large populations.

This regionalization, while certainly benefitting the technical level of medical care at the facility itself, has had a very shameful effect on surrounding communities. Persons of limited income who live more than just a few miles from the regional center find their medical care limited to those life threatening occasions when they must have medical care or die quickly. Small businesses in the outlying communities are forced to abandon portions of their operations because of monopolistic practices at the regional centers.

Most importantly, because medical care in and of itself must finally be an intensely personal matter between the patient, the patient's family and the medical community, which now is often over one hundred miles away, the medical relationship suffers. Visits are limited, symptoms may be missed and the direct care givers may never come to know the patient.

One of the largest medical centers of the free world is located at Piedras Negras, Mexico. This center serves great numbers of persons from El Paso to San Antonio to Brownsville as well as for several hundred miles into Mexico. It should not be assumed that the great impact of this hospital is attributable to any one factor. Perhaps the largest factor is that it serves two or three million persons in some of the poorest areas of North America.

But this service, welcome as it is, comes at large cost. First, the style of care and the numbers served make it necessary for many to be passed through the system without secondary and tertiary levels of care that are necessary. Second, great sums of money are brought into Piedras Negras both from Eagle Pass, across the river, and from other areas of extreme poverty.

Medical community and other business and institutional personnel who could be strong leaders in literally thousands of communities, lifting the level both of medical care and general livability, are concentrated in small areas. The wealthy communities become wealthier in many ways at the expense of the poorer communities.

The statistical data concerning health alone for these counties is disheartening. Half these counties had neither a practicing dentist or physician in 1975. At least two of the counties (Mora, New Mexico and Petroleum, Montana) did not have a registered nurse. Elliott, Kentucky, spent less than 2% of county per capita income on health care, compared with a national mean of about 7%. Births to mothers under age 20 ranges from 109% to 270% of the national mean.

Coupling these figures together, the probability that an expectant mother, for instance, will get good prenatal care in these communities is practically nil. The probability of early detection of crippling and deadly diseases may be even slimmer. Certainly, the probability of early and adequate health care can be linked easily to its availability to the poorest of the poor and the farthest of the far. Regionalization is a destroyer of the poorest of the poor.

From the employment figures, it is easy to note that few persons in these counties, apart from government workers, are employed by any industry that would probably include adequate health insurance and pension benefits for the workers.

There are some problems getting good figures for study. Mora County, New Mexico, for instance keeps almost no records because there is no money to pay for the research. What little money is allocated for the area by various agencies is typically given over to a regional study which relies solely on percentages and thus perpetuates the problem. The same is true with Conejos, Colorado and many other counties which have areas which lie outside Indian Reservations. Even good studies are extremely difficult.

From the standpoint of urban populations and their needs, this study shows a variety of issues that are approximately the same for both urban and rural populations. For example, the fiercely intense gathering of the resources and personnel of the medical community has exacerbated the general health needs of the poorest of the poor. It has allowed and even encouraged physicians, dentists, administrators and others who are in position to target their income potentials to move away from service to the poor to service of the wealthy (which includes, of course, those who have good insurance).

Additionally, it is relatively easy to move a clinic or hospital to another area as the population around the location loses income or status and income for the institution deteriorates. For instance, there is little significant medical care available for the community around Wesley Community Center in Phoenix yet the Phoenix metropolitan area has perhaps the highest ratio of extremely wealthy medical professionals of any major city on earth.

A rather glaring issue in the matter of health care is the certainty that as localized health care comes to be less and less of a reality, prevention and early detection of diseases such as cancer become more and more of a problem. Medical care, instead of coming at the first sign of illness or irregular bodily patterns, comes only when the disease has reached such a pattern that it is seen as life threatening.

When there is a nurse or some other basic health personnel living on the next block, or closely related to the patient, at least some initial questions may be raised. But when these persons are removed either to major centers in other parts of the city or to regional centers miles away, this prevention and early detection becomes more and more a problem for the poor.

The Changing Face
of
Migrant Labor

While on this assignment I became aware of a dramatic change in migrant labor patterns in recent years.

I grew up and began my adult years in communities that relied heavily on migrant laborers to work the fields and tend the livestock. In these communities, migrant laborers were a valuable resource. These workers could earn a fairly decent living through the summer months at least, and good workers were always able to find employment.

Wages for these workers (at least the wages paid to the contractors for the workers) were the same (and sometimes a little higher) wages everyone else received for doing the labor. Those of us who worked in the fields along with the migrants knew that these people were doing fairly well as far as hourly or piece-work wages.

But we also knew them as poor people. We understood that they migrated because there was no work either in Mexico or in the Rio Grande Valley. Rumors were that migrant workers could come to Idaho and Oregon and Washington, work six months, and spend the rest of the year in luxury in Eagle Pass or Del Rio.

As time went along, it was easy to see that things were changing, but I didn't know why. Some of these migrants didn't go back to Texas or to Piedras Negras. They stayed in the northern areas, getting permanent jobs at first in agribusiness, especially in food processing and marketing. The canned and frozen food processing developments made this change possible.

The most independent of these persons began to establish business ties in an area, coming back year after year. Many of the middle sized trucking firms of the northern tier of states were started by labor contractors who decided to settle down with their vehicles. First it was long term labor contracts, then bank accounts, and vehicle purchases, and eventually the children just entered school and they stayed all year.

Migrant labor became a more precious resource because the migrant patterns slowed to a trickle. We did not know why, so we attributed it to the rise of social service delivery systems that made it possible for these persons to survive without working. However, I have recently found some additional answers.

A large number of labor contractors of previous years no longer return to Eagle Pass and Del Rio for their workers. Recent immigration restrictions have dried up the route for workers simply coming across the river to work in the U.S. Machines have replaced hand work in many crops. These details were known to me already.

There are jobs in the Rio Grande Valley year round for as many workers as will go to the fields or into the processing plants. Only in June does the harvest slack off some. Families can stay in Crystal City or other areas and never have to leave for work. In fact, one farmer told me, behind closed doors, that he had to recruit illegals from Mexico through mutual acquaintances in order to have enough workers. The Del Monte plant in Crystal City is nearly always looking for workers.

Traveling is as much a matter of personal identity and pride as anything. It is a way of life, perhaps even a hobby, that gives persons the economic conditions they need to move around a good bit without embarrassing the family banker. One lady, Mrs. Noemi Cumpian, raised in a traveling family and traveling with her husband and small children, told me they finally felt almost forced to give it up. The children didn't want to travel that much. However, the chief difficulty was that the family was not certain they could afford to make the switch to a more settled life. The economic risk was great.

However, settle they did, and successfully. She is now the manager of the Texas State Employment Commission office in Crystal City.

Migrants (really, traveling workers) know they can make good incomes as families as they move about. Mrs. Cumprian talked about the many who purchase new or nearly new motor homes or personal vans in which to make the summer trips. There is a greater insistence by the children that the family return in time for the start of school. In some cases the children return early and stay with a relative until the parents choose to return.

The permanent migration of the "wealth makers", the labor contractors (contratistas, I believe) to other areas has left several areas of the Rio Grande Valley devoid of persons to establish new and stronger business patterns. Crystal City has particularly felt this.

The contractors found it very difficult to sign on workers during the time the La Raza Unida group managed the affairs of the County. One ex-contractor mentioned that during that period he simply stayed up north and worked in a food plant rather than face the frustration of trying to find workers. He is now retired and living again in Crystal City. "It's inexpensive to live here with the housing support and all." He would not give me his name.

What does this all mean to today's labor market in the northern and western states?

First, that the primary way to attract traveling workers is to treat them like tourists first. It means provision of nice (not just enclosed) lodging. It means selling the workers on community amenities, such as parks, and churches, and colleges, and scenery, and climate. It means contracting with ambitious persons to lead the "tours" of workers through a particular area. It means selling comfort as much as income.

Perhaps, most of all, it means seeing the workers in a completely different light. Communities will find that it pays big dividends to welcome them into the community, into churches, schools, groups, recreational facilities. This way was usually reserved in previous years for snow birds who come home to roost for the summer.

Second, in means that cultural and economic ties with border towns might be developed by northern communities. Sister city relationships, tourist packages, industrial packaging and cultural festivals must be shared both ways if the travelers are to be expected to keep coming. For instance, Sunnyside, Washington, could well be the sister city for Eagle Pass, Texas. There are probably as many adults living in Sunnyside who were born in Eagle Pass as were born in Sunnyside.

Third, that all the levels of the church must learn to treat the travelers as the valuable persons they really are rather than seeing them as a drain on the local economy. Actually, many local economies across the country have dried up when the travelers quit coming. These persons are to be evangelized, educated, motivated, and trained just as those who live a more sedate life.

Finally, northern and western states might find that beginning to treat these persons in a more respectful manner might just open the door for hundreds of thousands of other persons who would like to come to the area for a visit and to earn their way along. It seems likely that, if this picture were to develop more complete, many persons would be attracted to the traveling life, especially during the summer months. The Church might have a hand in promoting this possibility.

The thought of spending the summer traveling, earning perhaps $50-$200 per day per person (minimum wage would work out to about $35 per day, but most of the travelers I spoke with assumed an average of about $50 for women and about $75 for men), working out in the open, seeing the northern and western states, and returning hard and lean in the fall to a desk job or classroom, does not seem all that bad.

The Failure of the Church

Of all my findings in this project, this is the saddest and most difficult to write. It is a terrible thing to have a deep commitment to an institution and at the same time recognize that it is failing at its largest task.

It has become apparent to me that the Church could and should play a very large role in economic development in any given area. The church is always asking persons to give, give and give some more. Is it fair to always be asking persons to give without at the same time making it possible for them to create more wealth for themselves and others? I think not.

In fifty years of work in the Church it has become apparent to me that the greed and the desperate struggle for status in the world that too often drive the Church are the greatest enemies of its mission. Time after time in thirty years of professional ministry I have seen Christ betrayed by clergy and laity alike who seem to be interested only in what the Church can provide them. This self serving ministry of the Church can otherwise be described as competitive greed. Given this blotch on humanity, is it any wonder the church appears impotent and uncaring in the face of poverty?

One my first day of work at the General Board of Global Ministries one of my co-workers, Fred Heleine, took me aside to talk a little about the work. "Karl, the first thing you have to remember here is this. When you walk in that door down there on the street, you don't have a friend in the world. There is not a person here who would hesitate to slit your throat if it would advance their own career."

Over the next several years I learned the real truth to that statement. The primary function of the general agencies of any denomination (or group of demoninations) that I have seen is to provide employment for a group of politicians. Only the secondary function, that of serving God and God's people makes it worth while to tolerate spending money on the first.

The primary and secondary functions of the hierarchies of the Church is similar. They first provide both a means of gaining status within the world and a means of controlling the lives of others. Both these aims are clearly opposed to the work of Christ in the world. The world has seen enough of Wyatt Earp and Idi Amin.

But the secondary purpose, that of developing and maintaining the organizational structure and integrity of the Church, may make it worth while to live with the first. Most of the people in the various hierarchies do care. We could not have any organized religion without such structures.

The problem is that when we come together to work or to deal with social issues we become caught up in mob actions. The problem with original sin is that it is good at forcing its way to the fore when groups of people come together. At that time it is also reinforced by the greed and the drive for status and control. Then, as the saying goes, "All Hell breaks loose."

The Roman Catholic Church seems to be ineffectual in all these counties. In Conejos County, one Roman Catholic lay person, Mr. Herman Gallegos, highly influential in the community, spent fifteen minutes at a community meeting castigating his own congregation for not doing anything but grab the money and send it off to Rome. But his comments were not all just bitterness and grating waste of time. He made the following points, and his statements were seconded by most of the group in attendance.

A: The Church needs to recognize that Christ was not against poor people making money. In fact, Christ's principles of the disciplined life, inter-dependence, commitment to justice, and the value of the family are very beneficial when applied to the task of making wealth for persons.

B.   The Church knows how to train people to pray, and to preach, and to teach, and to sing, and to lie their way out of moral issues. Certainly the Church can teach people how to make wealth.

C.   It is not just to train persons to give their wealth to the Church without first training them to create wealth for themselves and for each other.

D.   The Church has huge financial resources, but if this man wants to start a knife-sharpening business, there is no possibility of borrowing the $100 from the Church.

E.   If all the Church can do with its emphasis on personal religion is to motivate persons to accept whatever is handed out, then Karl Marx was right. But if the Church, in the development of personal religious faith, will motivate persons to make personal changes for the better, including a better financial environment, then Karl Marx was wrong. That is the only choice.

F.   Finally, the Church is not doing a very good job right now developing trust in the integrity and justice and morality of institutions, including the Church. Obviously we were talking about Jim and Tammy Bakker and others, but Mr. Gallegos was also talking about his own congregation in a way that was hidden from me. I did not have a chance to check that out.

It appears that Jesus clearly believed that the principles and values he listed were important in all facets of life. Or, to perhaps say it better, no part of life can be separated finally from any other.

The Parable of the Talents and several of the others have long been known to speak to economic realities in life. What is not often clear is that the form of parable as Jesus used it is intended to hit as large an area of life as possible for the listener.

In parable, if one listens closely and from the heart, the response that typically comes is "Eh?" There is a call within the parable to enter the New Creation. We humans have a tendency to resist allowing every facet of our existence to be drawn into the Kingdom. Most use the terminology `Original Sin' for this phenomena. Some call it alienation. Jesus' parables make no allowance for the exclusion of any area from the Call.   Thus the puzzled, concerned and annoyed response to Christ. "Eh?"

Within the promise of Christ we are invited to find meaning in the Gospel story for every bit of one's life, because Christ came to deal with the totality of existence, not just the spiritual life of the human portion of the earth's denizens. The great message of the Church for all of life is that absolutely nothing is allowed to escape the Call to the New Creation.

All too frequently the Church itself separates off from the Call the portions of life with which it wishes not to be involved. That is certainly the case in all the counties I visited.

In most of these counties, the members of the local congregation pointed out that my visit to the county was the first sign ever of real involvement of the Church in their desperate lives.

Early on in the study I asked one pastor what he would say to a person who was considering going into business, and was struggling with whether or not it might be successful. The pastor's answer seemed to be standard for most of the pastors I spoke with in the study.

"I would remind them of Christ's call to give to the Church, and to share their wealth with the less fortunate. I would suggest that they might want to re-think their pledge to the church. I would ask them if there were some special project in which they were interested, and would like to support individually." !!!!

And we wonder why people leave the Church.

Most pastors do care. They just have not been taught what it is that they can do. One pastor confided with tears in his eyes that he saw his people become poorer every day and that he was powerless to stop it.

I believe that district superintendents care, but frequently misread the signs of the community and the congregation. Because the church tends to reflect the feelings of the community, most of these congregations have a good deal of turmoil and tension. Typically the pastor in the community is moved every year or two. The stated reason is usually "They just don't seem to be able to bring the church together."

It's a vicious cycle. The pastor doesn't know what is wrong, so tries to work on the symptoms. The symptoms are expressed in the way people relate to each other and to the pastor. The people don't know what is wrong, but the pastor is apparently attacking the things they hold dear. They complain to the district superintendent.

The district superintendent doesn't know what is wrong, but remembers that a few years ago the church was doing so well and then a change was made to reward a pastor that appeared to be doing well. Now with this pastor things are not good. The first responsibility of a district superintendent is the protection of the stability of the system. The Bishop is consulted. The only control the Bishop has is the appointment system. A new pastor is appointed who doesn't know what is wrong and.......

In the study I frequently asked people what, if anything, the church should be doing in economic development in the community. I heard all manner of answers from an embarrassed silence to protestations that it was no business of the Church because "God doesn't care how rich or poor you are".

Except where there has been a big public furor over some action by one denomination or another, denominational staff and hierarchy came in for only minor criticism from most people. This was probably for good reason. In some of the towns with United Methodist Churches I had to ask several persons before someone could point out where to find it. In one community there was not even a sign on the building or the grounds.

Most pastors I visited seemed to equate economic development with some sort of political action, and resisted any church involvement. When I began to mention that such things as self esteem, cooperation, tension, and impatience were issues for the Church the tone changed. "Well, yes, those are the work of the church, but economic development is not."

It appears that pastors need to be reminded that these factors are indeed the responsibility of the church and are specific mission targets. Only rarely did it seem that it would be profitable (in any way) for the congregation as a body to enter any kind of specific economic development project. It is far more important for the church to do what it does best, deal with relationships.

One answer was remarkably consistent from a specific group of people. I did not set my sights on this group early on, but they began to appear as if by magic--or a miracle. This was a group of business persons in every community who were either attempting to establish a business, had tried and failed, or had tried and succeeded. When I asked them the question of the involvement of the church the response was quite different.

"I wish I knew that God really wants me to succeed. I wish my pastor, with whom I spend more time than I do with my wife, would be a little bit encouraging about my business."

"I keep trying to tell myself that I'm good enough to make it in this business. Nobody else believes I can, I guess."

"My pastor told me a hundred times that it was important to try. If he hadn't, I wouldn't have tried at all."

"When I started my business I had to work late one night and miss a council meeting. I had been a member of that church all my life, but they decided that since I was now in business for myself, I wouldn't have time for the church. They elected someone that night to fill my position. I have never gone back." This statement was not from a United Methodist.

One man, from Crystal City, Texas, said "Isn't it a shame that the Church that takes such pride in having trained so many people to do things always takes someone who is already a success at business and puts them in the treasurer spot. Why not take a greenhorn and train them? It would make the whole world a better place."

None of the pastors I interviewed--of any denomination--had previously considered service in the church as being any kind of training for getting along in the world. It seemed as if the sole importance of the task in the congregation is to hold the congregation together, pay the apportionments, and present at least a minimal recording system at charge conference. It hardly seems worth it.

Leadership appears to be a result of training. In only a couple cases did I hear of local congregations doing anything that I would consider to be leadership training. In my own experience, leadership training has been offered by the Church only to those who were already in positions of leadership.

Why not take persons from the local community who perhaps have some unrealized potential and train them? Is it really necessary within the Church to train persons only for the paying of apportionments and rubber stamping the pastoral appointments?

Now that I am involved in starting a business I am acutely aware of this personal need for support from my church. In every sermon and prayer and song I listen for something that will sustain me or be usable in what I am trying to do. I usually listen in vain.

What is there that the preacher can and should lay out for the hungry parishioner? The most important statement is "You are, indeed, as valuable as every other human being on the face of the earth, past, present or future."

Time after time while doing this study some local entrepreneur or potential entrepreneur let me know that they felt God (particularly in the person of the Church) was letting them down. This disappointing message nearly always came in the lack of support for those persons who attempted to achieve something worthwhile in the community.

It often seemed that the pastor and denominational executives viewed the local commercial community as the opposition, a threat to the Church and its established (and I use that word carefully) position. Perhaps the Church has spent so much energy attacking greed and moral deprivation within the commercial structures that it cannot recognize righteousness within the same setting.

It should be noted that the General Board of Global Ministries did, at the time of the study, have a person working in the area of Economic Development. I have never seen his job description, but the only activities I have ever known him to be involved with center around teaching elderly women how to grow a window box garden. Nice, but not a particularly good use of $100,000 per year in salary and support costs. However, it does provide employment for him and his secretary. It also allows the Board to say "Yes, we are working in the area of economic development."

Another message eagerly sought by the commercial community is the acceptance of failure. Christ never condemned one who tries and fails. He only chastised those who never tried.

The Church has historically become so competitive within itself that economic or social or political failure is nearly universally seen as equivalent to spiritual condemnation. Within the Church, many who try and fail have been burned at the stake, defrocked, or appointed to the remotest outposts of the world. The message is clear: If acceptance by the hierarchy of the Church is important to you, do not try anything. This message is deadly for would-be entrepreneurs.

One problem with the pattern of throwing money at social ills concerns the National Program Division of the United Methodist Church more directly. In several of the counties the National Program Division has been involved with a variety of social services and issues. Sometimes this has been very positive. The work through the ecumenical organization in Alamosa, Colorado provides a great portion of the social services of Conejos County, but the people of Conejos County know very little of the involvement of the United Methodist Church in their lives.

The knowledge of denominational involvement is not always positive. In one county a man who (his pastor says) had personally requested help from the National Program Division to deal with a tight labor situation said to me, "The National Division came in here, took a quick look, decided I was the enemy because I was making money, and set about destroying me."

In another state a businessman said, "I quit the Church for a long time after that confrontation. The Church said it was wrong for me to make money even though I was giving half my net to the Church. I think the problem was that I knew how to make money and those cry babies who came down from New York didn't."

In county after county two conflicting images persist: one, that the Church in general and the United Methodist Church in particular believe making a profit to be wrong; and two, that the United Methodist Church believes those who are not wealthy have no value. Notice that these images only conflict. They are not mutually exclusive, and they may both be correct.

But for both these images to be correct, the denomination must make some very strange bedfellows. The Church must come to believe that it is a great sin to be wealthy. It must also believe that Christ came to seek and save the sinners. Interestingly, these are two of the great preaching themes of current Christian thought.

With these themes at hand, the Church can (and does) comfort itself by going after the really great sinners, the wealthiest people in the world. When it lands them, it celebrates.

When a famous actor or politician makes a profession of faith, the pastor is likely to release a press statement. When has a pastor ever mimeographed a statement such as this?

> "Maud Jones, a resident of Plaintown since birth, has today accepted Jesus as her personal savior. Ms. Jones, mother of three grown children, has worked thirty years in local restaurants and institutions in food service ministries. She currently resides in the Michael House, a home for elderly residents without resources.
>
> Ms. Jones spoke eloquently from the chancel rail of her deep faith and love of Christ. "Maybe because I have never been married, I have always dreamed there would be some one out there for me. I just did not know it was Jesus."
>
> The pastor, Dr. Hiram Bigheart, has announced the establishment of a special fund to commemorate the occasion. The proceeds of the fund will be used to provide food for needy families. The first contribution to the fund was from Ms. Jones herself, a gift of $7.23. Others who wish to contribute to the fund may send the contribution to......."

Whenever I found a person who said they no longer attended church I tried to find out why. The most common statement eventually came to be, "There's nothing there that is important to me right here and now. I am trying to feed my family, and the Church is trying to tell me that Jesus just does not care."

This is a powerful statement. It is particularly unsettling as we realize that we worship one who seemed to place an extremely strong emphasis on the power of persons coming together to make their lives better. The largest need in these areas is cooperative effort, utilizing all the resources available. Therefore it seems only fitting that the Church itself should be the leader in both teaching and implementing such cooperative effort. Yet almost every place I went, the Church was seen primarily as a place to escape responsibility for the current situation. If this is truthfully the manner in which the Church has positioned itself, it will obviously continue to die off in these areas, and rightfully so.

The persons in these communities were not making any wholesale attempts to escape their locations, or their ancestral homes, or their schools or businesses. They were only electing to search for ways to make their lives better. The Church, if it hears the Word of Christ at all, must not only heed this call but lead in the effort.

The most powerful response I heard from any person about the church came from a man who is a very successful farmer businessman. He teaches a church school class, occasionally preaches, and has held most of the major offices of the congregation. I asked him why.

He said, "Two reasons. First, I need it. I learn more than anyone else in the class. Second, the community needs it. I have learned some things in my life and I can share them this way. I can help people become rich in more ways than one."

Amen. I was thrilled with that response.

However, in 1992, it was reported on a television news program (60 Minutes) that this same man was accused of using the names of several poor families whose land he farmed to gain additional government subsidy payments. Then apparently none of this additional money was passed on to the families in whose name the subsidies were requested.

If this allegation is correct, is this the Church of Jesus, the Christ?

What questions can we legitimately and necessarily pursue in our support and our studies of these problems?

We need to keep talking with people in the churches, although this has been spotty at best. In Eagle Pass, I met with two different groups of people, and had asked for at least some persons with low income. In one meeting everyone in the room but the pastor and I made over $50,000 per year. In the other meeting, no one but the pastor and I made more than $10,000.

I had more luck finding poor people in the bars and restaurants and gas stations than in the churches. Of course, these conversations could not be scientifically recorded, but I did get most of my questions answered. I talked with perhaps 20 persons in these kinds of situations.

Overall, I probably had conversation of some depth with around 100 persons in one intense period of two weeks. Except in Mora County, the church is not the church of poor persons, but the sanctuary of the small band of middle class persons in the community. In Zavala, both "poor people's pastors" have been moved.

It is probably true that the greatest handicap to effective and creative ministry in these areas is the superintendency of the denomination. Somehow we must get to the superintendents and motivate them to be supportive and creative in their own ministry in order that the parish pastor be enabled to be supportive and creative in their own.

The Role of the Church

What can the Church do? Since this is where the project started, perhaps this is where it should end.

The Congregation

The Church has never taken seriously the possibility that evangelism is anything but a call to be one of Jesus' sheep. Of course, there is little fault in that, except that sheep are not particularly good leaders. Old buck sheep become cranky and mean occasionally, but violent aggression and responsible Christian leadership do not equate. Among sheep, someone has to be the goat to be a good leader.

The evangelism the Church has to offer is first a call to be fully human. That is, there are many otherwise well intentioned people in the world who try to be content in praying for the world and living in heaven. That process does not and can not work. We can only pray from the stance of the world, for that is who we are and where we live.

We all have to live in the world, taking our best shot at being responsible for life, both for our own and the lives of others. When we risk failure (and we will fail often if we are trying to accomplish anything) we know we are still loved and appreciated by God for we have tried to live out Jesus' mandates. God has not called us to be `little gods', but full human beings.

Second, the evangelism of Jesus is a call to be fully human in recognizing the goodness of our own and the lives of others. The Church is in a very unique position. It has the resources of community blessing and finances and prestige and training to say to the potential entrepreneurs in any community, "Go for it! God loves you and wants you to make it! It is important to all of us that you succeed, so we will help in every way we can."

Of course, this is a far cry from "When you make it, give me your money"!

The Church is a training ground. It could even be called a reform school for sinners. I firmly believe that as far as possible every office in the congregation should be held for a maximum of four years. We have a world of people out there who are begging for training in the skills of organization and business, and churches full of people who know so much about their task they have not even thought about it in ten years. Recruiting and training new workers must be a crucial part of any evangelistic effort that claims to be supportive of economic development.

The Church can train in finances, in budgeting, in organization, in computers, in service product development, in time line management and in employee relations. After two thousand years, the Church ought to have its house in order in salesmanship and in public relations. It ought to know (and does!) how to advertise, how to bring people to the showroom (church activities), help them decide on an appropriate purchase, and offer a lifetime warranty on its services.

Of course, emphases in these areas would require our seminaries to take the congregation and its operations seriously as support for the community economy, perhaps for a change. A two hour course in church management as a satisfactory preparation for a professional degree is a disgrace to all of us, and particularly to Jesus. Where are the courses that train forthcoming pastors to train laity in sales, and in finances, and in planning, and in warranty support?

When operating at its best the Church has always fostered the creative juices of the world. The greatest art, the wildest scientific concepts and the strangest words have all come about in part because of the interaction of persons with the Church. It is no accident that in the various communities of this study the churches that were recognized as the strongest were those that spent a lot of time driving the life of the community. They gained their prestige not by holding great spiritual revivals, but by presenting plays, holding community dream sessions, even playing ROOK on Friday nights.

Life in the communities with the weakest economies can become quite stale. Discouragement is the overdrawn checkbook of community life. It has to be balanced by heroic acts on someone's part. The great call of the Lord is to put the minds and hearts of the people to some task that just might bring about a better life for them.

Part of the genius of Jesus is that he called us to a better life without spelling out every detail. He just assumed, and rightfully so, that given a little support, we could figure it out for ourselves. Creativity can be fostered in many ways by the local congregation. That talent will then be put to use in the community as the people work for a better life.

The Larger Church Organization
(Denominational Structure)

In addition to the efforts mentioned above, there are some specific ways for the denomination to help. The reasons these must be taken on by the larger church have mostly to do with the cost in personal power, prestige, and actual dollars.

The first of these steps is that the Church absolutely must begin to recruit and train appropriate pastors for this work, and reward them properly for their commitment. As a general rule, pastors of these congregations turn out to be the lowest paid pastors in the area, living in the poorest house, and driving the oldest cars. For those reasons alone, the typical pastor in this work is either very young or very old, either just getting started or just filling out time in retirement.

Some means must be found of encouraging pastors to train specifically for this work and to push the Superintendents into leaving them there long enough to do some good. One simple means of doing this would be to establish the payments of the denomination into the pastor's retirement fund based on the per capita income of the community. The mean per capita income of the judicatory (conference, district, etc) is easy to establish. The standard rate of pension investment would be made for pastors serving any communities at that level. Then, if the community has a higher income, the payments are less. If the community has a lower income, the payments are more. Certainly, a pastor serving a 1,500 member congregation and making $80,000 to $100,000 in total remuneration as many are today has a much easier time preparing for retirement than a pastor serving a congregation at Rio Grande City, Texas, and making a total of $15,000 per year.

A second portion of the work of the larger organization is in the appointment (or call) of pastors for these areas. Everyone must understand that these are special congregations, and cannot be dealt with in the way bureaucracies like to work. By their very nature there will be enormous conflicts within because the people are hurting. If there is no hope for better life, people fight.

Most superintendents and bishops forget this at appointment time. The very act of pulling a pastor out of a congregation that is fighting because of its economic pattern kills whatever hope is left. If the pastor wants to stay, and is apparently doing a decent job, the superintendent has the obligation to make if feasible for the pastor to stay. However, in most cases the superintendent does not really have a clue.

Most episcopal visits to the counties of this study had occurred some ten to fifteen years apart. District Superintendents often make their annual visits as ninety minute annual meetings, refusing even to stay overnight in a local home or motel. One district superintendent I know even drove four hours after such a meeting. He just did not want to stay in the community that night.

The Church, taken as a whole, has enormous resources available for economic support. Many billions of dollars are held by the Church in a variety of forms not particularly useful in other ways except to make more money. Retirement funds, real estate, and jewelry do not seem to be particularly necessary beyond a certain point for the support of the hierarchy necessary for the preaching of the Word.

It would seem quite feasible to use some of that enormous hoard. The Church could loan it (not give, except in rarest necessity), interest free, to entrepreneurs in the various counties to start new businesses. Actually, I suspect it would be returned many times over by successful new businesses.

I think perhaps Jesus may have said something about just that issue.

Perhaps just as important, the Church could take some of that money and spread the word to its people, saying "Go there and spend money. Get to know the people there. Build the community of Christ, and spend money. Purchase some books from the little general store at Sandy Hook, Kentucky. Go to worship at the church in Tselani, Arizona. Drop some money in the collection plate."

Many persons, of course, will never have the opportunity to visit any of these counties. However that may be, they can still participate in mission to these counties as a congregation and as individuals. Let me make some suggestions, both for individuals and for church committees, groups, circles and classes.

A congregation might take on as a sister congregation one in one of these counties. It does not even need necessarily to be of the same denomination or faith group. Financial assistance, personal contacts and relationships, even just information about the county and involvement in its life are important.

An individual can make personal contact with the area. It is a simply matter to subscribe to the weekly paper in Sandy Hook or Tunica or Window Rock. For a few dollars a veritable fountain of up to date information about and personal contact with each area is available.

Every area has possibilities of economic growth, particularly for businesses that might choose to come to the area. Individuals and congregations can and should begin to provide incentive in the form of information, encouragement and even pressure for companies in which they have an interest to settle in these areas.

Letters and phone calls to media persons, including radio and television personalities, lifting up the possibilities of these counties for both visiting land for business are very inexpensive.

Words to acquaintances about visiting the areas and spending money there is certainly an inexpensive hobby. Even contributions to the churches in these counties are very welcome. If possible, though, it is important to go to the county and visit it personally.

If the Church will take its mission seriously, sending persons into these areas, these counties will recover. Consider that the United Methodist Church has over eight million members. Additionally, there are another eight million who are somehow connected to the church, constituents. Sixteen million persons whom I believe are eager to do practical and efficient mission work.

If somehow five percent (one out of twenty) United Methodist members and constituents simply paid a visit to at least one of these counties, there would be a true miracle. If they spend only $100 each, that total direct money would be $80,000,000. After the money has replicated itself within the counties as the people go about their daily lives, that amount would be over $200,000,000. And if those who go tell their friends, who get their own churches involved.......? Mission on the cheap! That almost sounds to be a contradiction in terms for any denomination. An inexpensive miracle!

Sometimes the Church sends mission teams to these areas. This happens especially to Kentucky to communities of the Redbird Missionary Conference. The concept is good, but what generally happens? Most often, some congregation or another sends a team of workers into the county to add a room on to the church, or paint the sanctuary.

Do they go with cash? Certainly not. That would be too easy. Where do they buy the paint? Someplace else.

Where do they buy the lumber? They bring it in by truck from someplace else.

Where do they buy the food? They bring it from home. Often they even show up with motor homes (so they won't have to stay in a motel or in folks' homes) carrying enough fuel to get them back up to Lexington before the tank runs dry.

And what happens? They literally destroy the remaining self esteem of the local congregation by bringing in their "stuff", as if the local supplies are not good enough. They arrive, snap a few pictures of the dreadful poverty, do their work and leave without getting to know the local business people. They go away feeling superior to "those poor people", which they are not.

Because the general economic climate of the each area will be better, the additional business picked up by the affected enterprises should more than make up for the initial shift of economy to the poorest areas. When the economy looks more viable in an area, more persons will want in on the action. When the folks in the poorest counties have a little more money, they are going to spend it both locally and in the surrounding communities.

Now, out of those redirected millions, approximately one third will finally end up in taxes paid to city, county, state and federal governments. A few million in increased tax revenue from increased commercial activity, even spread over twenty five counties, will provide many services for those residents.

Additionally, the increase in contributions to local charitable and spiritual organizations, churches, fraternal orders and other causes will increase greatly as the local community has more money. This will relieve the necessity of relying on outside charity money to relieve the grinding poverty of the county. Also, the burden on the tax pile to make welfare payments will be eased.

There are a great many intangible benefits to be gained from this as well. The self esteem of the local residents will be lifted as a result of having been able to succeed in operating a business. This new self image will promote additional efforts by the entire community as it witnesses the success of its efforts.

Second, as new services and markets are opened, residents will be able to shop and spend locally. New specialty shops will spring up, both to attract the tourist dollars and to serve the needs of the locals.

Third, as the new services and markets are opened, a great new sense of the value of education will come to the community. Both in the mixing with and understanding of the visitors from the outside world, and in the drive to make the best use of the dollars now coming into the pocket, education will be a valuable commodity. Where there is no hope, education is not taken seriously. Education only becomes valuable when there is hope.

Then, as more persons become familiar with the county and its possibilities, some will choose to make it their home. Some will choose to develop new industries in the area. Some will choose to retire in these underutilized resort areas such as Mora, New Mexico and Conejos, Colorado and Monticello, Utah. (These just happen to have fine skiing conditions and resorts.)

Much more can be done in many new and creative ways. Most important, most critical, and easiest is the simple practice called for to truly alleviate the poverty that exists in all these counties:

Go There And Spend Money

Appendix I
Additional County Trends

These counties are among the initial list of 25. I did not get to visit these other counties. Some were visited by other members of the team. The only additional data that is of particular importance here is that a total of eight (nearly one third) of the total study counties are basically populated by Native Americans. These people hold approximately the same status in the U.S. as did the Canaanites of Old Testament times.

Shannon County, South Dakota shares with Mora County, New Mexico the dubious honor of being the poorest counties in the nation. Mora County seems to be making some progress. Shannon County almost seems to be a lost cause, particularly in the eyes of the federal government and the Church.

Buffalo, South Dakota   Trend Information
Population and Households   Native American

	1970	1980	% Chg	1986	% Chg	1991	% Chg	
	Census	Census	70-80	(Est.)	80-86	(Proj.)	86-91	
Population	1739	1795	3.2	1667	-7.1	1558	-6.5	
Households	411	445	8.3	425	-4.5	408	-4.0	
Household Size	4.18*	4.03	-3.4	3.92	-2.8	3.82	-2.6	
Group Quarters	0	0	0.0	0	0.0			
Income	1969	1979	% Chg	1986	% Chg	1991	% Chg	
	Census	Census	69-79	(Est.)	79-86	(Proj.)	86-91	
Agg. Income($mm)	2.9	4.7	61.2	5.6	17.1	5.8	3.8	
Per Capita ($)	1692	2642	56.1	3332	26.1	3700	11.0	
Average Hh ($)	7122	10613	49.0	13014	22.6	14077	8.2	
Median Hh ($)	5020	9691	93.0	11399	17.6	12267	7.6	
Household	Income		Distribution					
	1979		1986		1991			
	Count	%	Count	%	Count	%		
Less than $ 7,500	175	39.3	147	34.6	129	31.6		
$ 7,500 - $14,999	165	37.1	126	29.6	118	28.9		
$15,000 - $24,999	74	16.6	98	23.1	96	23.5		
$25,000 - $34,999	29	6.5	37	8.7	43	10.5		
$35,000 - $49,999	2	0.4	17	4.0	20	4.9		
$50,000 - $74,999	0	0.0	0	0.0	2	0.5		
$75,000 and over	0	0.0	0	0.0	0	0.0		

*1970 Household Size Is an Estimate Based on 1970 Census Data.
Data on Income Are Expressed in "Current" Dollars for Each Respective Year.
Hh=household   Agg=aggregate

Corson, South Dakota   Trend Information
Population and Households   Native American

	1970	1980	% Chg	1986	% Chg	1991	% Chg
	Census	Census	70-80	(Est.)	80-86	(Proj.)	86-91
Population	4994	5196	4.0	5161	-0.7	5129	-0.6
Households	1280	1449	13.2	1481	2.2	1512	2.1
Household Size	3.87*	3.51	-9.2	3.42	-2.8	3.32	-2.7
Group Quarters	103	103	0.0	103	0.0		
Income	1969	1979	% Chg	1986	% Chg	1991	% Chg
	Census	Census	69-79	(Est.)	79-86	(Proj.)	86-91
Agg. Income($mm)	8.3	18.3	121.4	20.8	13.9	23.5	12.9
Per Capita ($)	1655	3521	112.7	4038	14.7	4586	13.6
Average Hh ($)	6399	12750	99.2	13574	6.5	14868	9.5
Median Hh ($)	5354	10160	89.8	11421	12.4	12597	10.3
Household	Income		Distribution				
	1979		1986		1991		
	Count	%	Count	%	Count	%	
Less than $ 7,500	569	39.3	501	33.8	453	30.0	
$ 7,500 - $14,999	375	25.9	372	25.1	373	24.7	
$15,000 - $24,999	275	19.0	266	18.0	277	18.3	
$25,000 - $34,999	122	8.4	146	9.9	159	10.5	
$35,000 - $49,999	46	3.2	65	4.4	94	6.2	
$50,000 - $74,999	28	1.9	34	2.3	42	2.8	
$75,000 and over	1	0.1	7	0.5	15	1.0	

*1970 Household Size Is an Estimate Based on 1970 Census Data.

Data on Income Are Expressed in "Current" Dollars for Each Respective Year.

Hh=household Agg=aggregate

Dewey, South Dakota   Trend Information
Population and Households   Native American

	1970	1980	% Chg	1986	% Chg	1991	% Chg
	Census	Census	70-80	(Est.)	80-86	(Proj.)	86-91
Population	5170	5366	3.8	5521	2.9	5641	2.2
Households	1325	1531	15.5	1624	6.1	1704	4.9
Household Size	3.87*	3.48	-10.0	3.38	-3.0	3.29	-2.6
Group Quarters	34	34	0.0	34	0.0		
Income	1969	1979	% Chg	1986	% Chg	1991	% Chg
	Census	Census	69-79	(Est.)	79-86	(Proj.)	86-91
Agg. Income($mm)	8.8	21.2	139.5	25.3	19.5	29.4	16.4
Per Capita ($)	1709	3943	130.7	4580	16.2	5217	13.9
Average Hh ($)	6654	13601	104.4	15351	12.9	16898	10.1
Median Hh ($)	5258	11305	115.0	12691	12.3	13917	9.7
Household	Income		Distribution				
	1979		1986		1991		
	Count	%	Count	%	Count	%	
Less than $ 7,500	520	34.0	486	29.9	455	26.7	
$ 7,500 - $14,999	472	30.8	471	29.0	464	27.2	
$15,000 - $24,999	365	23.8	399	24.6	422	24.8	
$25,000 - $34,999	114	7.4	174	10.7	221	13.0	
$35,000 - $49,999	30	2.0	57	3.5	95	5.6	
$50,000 - $74,999	24	1.6	25	1.5	30	1.8	
$75,000 and over	6	0.4	12	0.7	17	1.0	

*1970 Household Size Is an Estimate Based on 1970 Census Data.
Data on Income Are Expressed in "Current" Dollars for Each Respective Year.
Hh=household   Agg=aggregate

Douglas, South Dakota   Trend Information
Population and Households   Anglo American

	1970	1980	% Chg	1986	% Chg	1991	% Chg
	Census	Census	70-80	(Est.)	80-86	(Proj.)	86-91
Population	4569	4181	-8.5	3843	-8.1	3554	-7.5
Households	1383	1425	3.0	1349	-5.3	1279	-5.2
Household Size	3.23*	2.87	-11.3	2.78	-3.1	2.70	-2.7
Group Quarters	98	98	0.0	98	0.0		
Income	1969	1979	% Chg	1986	% Chg	1991	% Chg
	Census	Census	69-79	(Est.)	79-86	(Proj.)	86-91
Agg. Income($mm)	7.8	15.0	102.6	18.0	14.3	18.4	2.0
Per Capita ($)	1705	3774	121.3	4695	24.4	5177	10.3
Average Hh ($)	5560	10885	95.8	13100	20.3	14052	7.3
Median Hh ($)	4656	9279	99.3	11223	21.0	12002	6.9
Household	Income		Distribution				
	1979		1986		1991		
	Count	%	Count	%	Count	%	
Less than $ 7,500	603	42.3	469	34.8	409	32.0	
$ 7,500 - $14,999	468	32.8	414	30.7	384	30.0	
$15,000 - $24,999	249	17.5	292	21.6	287	22.4	
$25,000 - $34,999	78	5.5	115	8.5	126	9.9	
$35,000 - $49,999	14	1.0	43	3.2	53	4.1	
$50,000 - $74,999	13	0.9	10	0.7	13	1.0	
$75,000 and over	0	0.0	6	0.4	7	0.5	

*1970 Household Size Is an Estimate Based on 1970 Census Data.
Data on Income Are Expressed in "Current" Dollars for Each Respective Year.
Hh=household Agg=aggregate

Harding, South Dakota   Trend Information
Population and Households   Anglo American

	1970	1980	% Chg	1986	% Chg	1991	% Chg
	Census	Census	70-80	(Est.)	80-86	(Proj.)	86-91
Population	1855	1700	-8.4	1974	16.1	2200	11.4
Households	547	582	6.4	701	20.4	803	14.6
Household Size	3.32*	2.83	-14.7	2.74	-3.2	2.67	-2.4
Group Quarters	53	53	0.0	53	0.0		
Income	1969	1979	% Chg	1986	% Chg	1991	% Chg
	Census	Census	69-79	(Est.)	79-86	(Proj.)	86-91
Agg. Income($mm)	4.1	8.7	112.7	9.1	4.7	12.3	35.1
Per Capita ($)	2211	5132	132.1	4628	-9.8	5612	21.3
Average Hh ($)	7363	14581	98.0	12659	-13.2	14975	18.3
Median Hh ($)	5844	12994	122.3	11067	-14.8	12956	17.1
Household	Income		Distribution				
	1979		1986		1991		
	Count	%	Count	%	Count	%	
Less than $ 7,500	165	28.4	243	34.7	232	28.9	
$ 7,500 - $14,999	173	29.7	226	32.2	233	29.0	
$15,000 - $24,999	146	25.1	157	22.4	196	24.4	
$25,000 - $34,999	65	11.2	49	7.0	90	11.2	
$35,000 - $49,999	24	4.1	20	2.9	37	4.6	
$50,000 - $74,999	9	1.5	6	0.9	13	1.6	
$75,000 and over	0	0.0	0	0.0	2	0.2	

*1970 Household Size Is an Estimate Based on 1970 Census Data.
Data on Income Are Expressed in "Current" Dollars for Each Respective Year.
Hh=household   Agg=aggregate

Mellette South Dakota   Trend Information
Population and Households   Native American

	1970	1980	% Chg	1986	% Chg	1991	% Chg
	Census	Census	70-80	(Est.)	80-86	(Proj.)	86-91
Population	2418	2249	-7.0	2415	7.4	2551	5.6
Households	664	685	3.2	756	10.4	822	8.7
Household Size	3.64*	3.22	-11.6	3.14	-2.6	3.05	-2.8
Group Quarters	44	44	0.0	44	0.0		
Income	1969	1979	% Chg	1986	% Chg	1991	% Chg
	Census	Census	69-79	(Est.)	79-86	(Proj.)	86-91
Agg. Income($mm)	4.6	8.1	73.3	9.9	22.6	11.8	19.8
Per Capita ($)	1922	3581	86.3	4089	14.2	4639	13.5
Average Hh ($)	6752	11798	74.7	13053	10.6	14333	9.8
Median Hh ($)	5607	9681	72.7	10918	12.8	12037	10.2
Household	Income	Distribution					
	1979		1986		1991		
	Count	%	Count	%	Count	%	
Less than $ 7,500	271	39.6	261	34.5	253	30.8	
$ 7,500 - $14,999	177	25.8	192	25.4	205	24.9	
$15,000 - $24,999	134	19.6	142	18.8	159	19.3	
$25,000 - $34,999	37	5.4	60	7.9	77	9.4	
$35,000 - $49,999	24	3.5	32	4.2	44	5.4	
$50,000 - $74,999	3	0.4	10	1.3	15	1.8	
$75,000 and over	0	0.0	0	0.0	1	0.1	

*1970 Household Size Is an Estimate Based on 1970 Census Data.
Data on Income Are Expressed in "Current" Dollars for Each Respective Year.
Hh=household Agg=aggregate

Shannon, South Dakota   Trend Information
Population and Households   Native American

	1970	1980	% Chg	1986	% Chg	1991	% Chg
	Census	Census	70-80	(Est.)	80-86	(Proj.)	86-91
Population	8198	11323	38.1	11179	-1.3	11042	-1.2
Households	1679	2306	37.3	2345	1.7	2379	1.4
Household Size	4.79*	4.84	1.0	4.70	-2.9	4.58	-2.7
Group Quarters	158	158	0.0	158	0.0		
Income	1969	1979	% Chg	1986	% Chg	1991	% Chg
	Census	Census	69-79	(Est.)	79-86	(Proj.)	86-91
Agg. Income($mm)	11.6	29.9	157.2	36.3	21.5	41.4	14.0
Per Capita ($)	1416	2637	86.2	3244	23.0	3745	15.4
Average Hh ($)	6841	12857	87.9	15404	19.8	17351	12.6
Median Hh ($)	5291	10533	99.1	12538	19.0	13915	11.0
Household	Income		Distribution				
	1979		1986		1991		
	Count	%	Count	%	Count	%	
Less than $ 7,500	894	38.8	752	32.1	672	28.2	
$ 7,500 - $14,999	638	27.7	626	26.7	605	25.4	
$15,000 - $24,999	556	24.1	559	23.8	558	23.5	
$25,000 - $34,999	132	5.7	273	11.6	327	13.7	
$35,000 - $49,999	33	1.4	72	3.1	144	6.1	
$50,000 - $74,999	29	1.3	28	1.2	32	1.3	
$75,000 and over	24	1.0	35	1.5	41	1.7	

*1970 Household Size Is an Estimate Based on 1970 Census Data.

Data on Income Are Expressed in "Current" Dollars for Each Respective Year.

Hh=household Agg=aggregate

Todd, South Dakota   Trend Information

Population and Households   Native American

	1970	1980	% Chg	1986	% Chg	1991	% Chg
	Census	Census	70-80	(Est.)	80-86	86-91	(Proj.)
Population	6606	7328	10.9	7318	-0.1	7297	-0.3
Households	1481	1877	26.7	1932	2.9	1977	2.3
Household Size	4.40*	3.87	-12.1	3.75	-3.0	3.66	-2.6
Group Quarters	69	69	0.0	69	0.0		
Income	1969	1979	% Chg	1986	% Chg	1991	% Chg
	Census	Census	69-79	(Est.)	79-86	Proj	86-91
Agg. Income($mm)	9.6	23.1	141.7	29.7	28.4	33.3	11.9
Per Capita ($)	1450	3159	117.9	4063	28.6	4558	12.2
Average Hh ($)	6427	11801	83.6	14695	24.5	16068	9.3
Median Hh ($)	5661	9828	73.6	12381	26.0	13403	8.3
Household	Income		Distribution				
	1979		1986		1991		
	Count	%	Count	%	Count	%	
Less than $ 7,500	782	41.7	638	33.0	591	29.9	
$ 7,500 - $14,999	501	26.7	504	26.1	505	25.5	
$15,000 - $24,999	429	22.9	431	22.3	437	22.1	
$25,000 - $34,999	119	6.3	245	12.7	269	13.6	
$35,000 - $49,999	35	1.9	87	4.5	136	6.9	
$50,000 - $74,999	0	0.0	16	0.8	27	1.4	
$75,000 and over	11	0.6	11	0.6	12	0.6	

*1970 Household Size Is an Estimate Based on 1970 Census Data.

Data on Income Are Expressed in "Current" Dollars for Each Respective Year.

Hh=household   Agg=aggregate

Ziebach, South Dakota   Trend Information

Population and Households   Native American

	1970	1980	% Chg	1986	% Chg	1991	% Chg
	Census	Census	70-80	(Est.)	80-86	(Proj.)	86-91
Population	2221	2308	3.9	2583	11.9	2808	8.7
Households	523	600	14.7	692	15.3	772	11.6
Household Size	4.25*	3.85	-9.4	3.73	-3.0	3.64	-2.6
Group Quarters	0	0	0.0	0	0.0		
Income	1969	1979	% Chg	1986	% Chg	1991	% Chg
	Census	Census	69-79	(Est.)	79-86	(Proj.)	86-91
Agg. Income($mm)	3.7	7.0	91.4	8.4	20.3	10.3	21.7
Per Capita ($)	1652	3042	84.1	3271	7.5	3662	12.0
Average Hh ($)	6904	11435	65.6	11805	3.2	12889	9.2
Median Hh ($)	5301	9474	78.7	8566	-9.6	9648	12.6
Household	Income		Distribution				
	1979		1986		1991		
	Count	%	Count	%	Count	%	
Less than $ 7,500	245	40.8	319	46.1	323	41.8	
$ 7,500 - $14,999	210	35.0	190	27.5	220	28.5	
$15,000 - $24,999	85	14.2	105	15.2	127	16.5	
$25,000 - $34,999	30	5.0	35	5.1	47	6.1	
$35,000 - $49,999	24	4.0	33	4.8	37	4.8	
$50,000 - $74,999	2	0.3	5	0.7	13	1.7	
$75,000 and over	4	0.7	5	0.7	5	0.6	

*1970 Household Size Is an Estimate Based on 1970 Census Data.
Data on Income Are Expressed in "Current" Dollars for Each Respective Year.
Hh=household   Agg=aggregate

Sioux, North Dakota   Trend Information

Population and Households   Native American

	1970	1980	% Chg	1986	% Chg	1991	% Chg
	Census	Census	70-80	(Est.)	80-86	(Proj.)	86-91
Population	3632	3620	-0.3	3750	3.6	3850	2.7
Households	824	920	11.7	983	6.8	1041	5.9
Household Size	4.35*	3.81	-12.5	3.70	-2.9	3.59	-3.0
Group Quarters	116	116	0.0	116	0.0		
Income	1969	1979	% Chg	1986	% Chg	1991	% Chg
	Census	Census	69-79	(Est.)	79-86	(Proj.)	86-91
Agg. Income($mm)	5.2	13.2	153.5	16.6	26.1	20.7	24.2
Per Capita ($)	1432	3642	154.3	4434	21.7	5366	21.0
Average Hh ($)	6266	14475	131.0	17227	19.0	20202	17.3
Median Hh ($)	5722	11959	109.0	14055	17.5	16631	18.3

Household	Income		Distribution				
	1979		1986		1991		
	Count	%	Count	%	Count	%	
Less than $ 7,500	306	33.3	273	27.8		244	23.4
$ 7,500 - $14,999	255	27.7	250	25.4		238	22.9
$15,000 - $24,999	213	23.2	229	23.3		236	22.7
$25,000 - $34,999	90	9.8	129	13.1		155	14.9
$35,000 - $49,999	39	4.2	68	6.9		107	10.3
$50,000 - $74,999	11	1.2	24	2.4		43	4.1
$75,000 and over	6	0.7	10	0		18	1.7

*1970 Household Size Is an Estimate Based on 1970 Census Data.

Data on Income Are Expressed in "Current" Dollars for Each Respective Year.

Hh=household Agg=aggregate

Petroleum, Montana   Trend Information

Population and Households   Anglo American

	1970	1980	% Chg	1986	% Chg	1991	% Chg
	Census	Census	70-80	(Est.)	80-86	(Proj.)	86-91
Population	675	655	-3.0	676	3.2	692	2.4
Households	225	232	3.1	247	6.5	260	5.3
Household Size	3.00*	2.82	-5.9	2.74	-3.1	2.66	-2.8
Group Quarters	0	0	0.0	0	0.0		
Income	1969	1979	% Chg	1986	% Chg	1991	% Chg
	Census	Census	69-79	(Est.)	79-86	(Proj.)	86-91
Agg. Income($mm)	1.6	3.6	127.6	3.0	-15.7	3.6	18.6
Per Capita ($)	2346	5502	134.5	4494	-18.3	5207	15.9
Average Hh ($)	7039	14904	111.7	11833	-20.6	13349	12.8
Median Hh ($)	6644	9821	47.8	7017	-28.6	8206	16.9

Household	Income		Distribution			
	1979		1986		1991	
	Count	%	Count	%	Count	%
Less than $ 7,500	90	38.8	132	53.4	122	46.9
$ 7,500 - $14,999	84	36.2	76	30.8	85	32.7
$15,000 - $24,999	34	14.7	24	9.7	36	13.8
$25,000 - $34,999	9	3.9	2	0.8	5	1.9
$35,000 - $49,999	2	0.9	4	1.6	2	0.8
$50,000 - $74,999	5	2.2	3	1.2	3	1.2
$75,000 and over	8	3.4	6	2.4	7	2.7

*1970 Household Size Is an Estimate Based on 1970 Census Data.
Data on Income Are Expressed in "Current" Dollars for Each Respective Year.
Hh=household   Agg=aggregate

Appendix II
Church Data

The data in the following tables reflects only United Methodist operations and activities in the various counties. This data is probably quite similar to that of other groups. Therefore no one should read into this portion of the book that the United Methodist Church is any better or worse than any other group for any area. That is a judgement for the people of the counties, not for the author.

This data is taken from various issues of the General Minutes of the Conferences of the United Methodist Church. The first row of numbers lists the column from which the data is quoted. The first column of numbers is a handy means of tracking a particular parish through the tables. Where no data is listed, none is listed in the Minutes.

United Methodist Churches. These churches are reflected by the data in the following tables.

Source: General Minutes of the Annual Conferences

#	County	State	Charge	Annual Conf.
1	Apache	Arizona	Window Rock	New Mexico
2	Lee	Arkansas	Marianna	No. Arkansas
3	Lee	Arkansas	Livingston	No. Arkansas
4	Lee	Arkansas	Mt Zion	No. Arkansas
5	Lee	Arkansas	Scruggs Chapel	No. Arkansas
6	Lee	Arkansas	Smiths Chapel	No. Arkansas
7	Conejos	Colorado	(No UMC)	Rocky Mountain
8	Elliott	Kentucky	Sandy Hook	Kentucky
9	Owsley	Kentucky	Booneville	Red Bird
10	McCreary	Kentucky	Whitley City	Kentucky
11	McCreary	Kentucky	Pleasant Run	Kentucky
12	Jefferson	Mississippi	Fayette	Mississippi
13	Jefferson	Mississippi	Fayette Ct.	Mississippi
14	Tunica	Mississippi	Tunica	No. Mississippi
15	Petroleum	Montana	NA	Yellowstone
16	Mora	New Mexico	(No UMC)	New Mexico
17	Sioux	No Dakota	(No UMC)	No. Dakota
18	Buffalo	So Dakota	(No UMC)	So. Dakota
19	Corson	So Dakota	(No UMC)	So. Dakota
20	Dewey	So Dakota	Timber Lake	So. Dakota
21	Douglas	So Dakota	NA	So. Dakota
22	Harding	So Dakota	Camp Crook	So. Dakota
23	Harding	So Dakota	Harding	So. Dakota
24	Mellette	So Dakota	(No UMC)	So. Dakota
25	Todd	So Dakota	Todd-Mellette	So. Dakota
26	Shannon	So Dakota	(No UMC)	So. Dakota
27	Ziebach	So Dakota	(No UMC)	So. Dakota
28	Hancock	Tennessee	Sneedville	Holston
29	Zavala	Texas	Crystal City	SW Texas
30	Zavala	Texas	Crys'l-Swindall	Rio Grande
31	Maverick	Texas	Eagle Pass	SW Texas
32	Maverick	Texas	Eagle' Trinidad	Rio Grande
33	Starr	Texas	Rio Grande City	SW Texas
34	Starr	Texas	Rio Grande City	Rio Grande
35	San Juan	Utah	Four Corners	Rocky Mountain

#Column	1976 Full Members Last year	1982 Full Members Last year	1976 Rec'd or Restored Members	1982 Rec'd or Restored Members	1976 Rec'd by Transfer	1982 Rec'd by Transfer
#Column	3	3	4	4	5	5
1	37	19	1	3		
2	597	561	6	1	10	4
3	191	30	8			3
4	15					
5	64					
6	13					
7						
8	156	50	1	92		8
9	306	201		7		1
10	196	124	1		6	2
11		65		1		6
12	336	253	1		4	
13	90	124	15		4	
14	603	579	6	3	12	3
15		41				
16						
17						
18						
19						
20	133	87	4	4		5
21						
22	26	27		1	3	2
23		10				
24						
25	230	179	4	2	6	5
26						
27						
28	304	254	1	1		5
29	231	133		1	1	
30	201				12	.
31	194	165	7		10	3
32	62				1	
33		44				1
34	301				5	
35						
Total:	4194	3038	55	116	74	48

#	1976 Removed All Ways	1982 Removed All Ways	1976 Members Death	1982 Members Death	1976 Total Full Members	1982 Total Full Members
#	6	6	7	7	8	8
1	2	1	2		36	21
2	13	10	10	8	590	548
3			1		194	33
4		15				
5						64
6						13
7						
8	15		1	2	141	148
9		1	4	6	302	202
10	3		1		199	126
11				2		70
12	6		3	4	332	249
13	5		2	1	102	123
14	6	12	5	7	610	566
15						
16						
17						
18						
19						
20	25	1		1	112	94
21						
22	3	9			26	21
23						10
24						
25	4	4	1	2	235	180
26						
27						
28	1	45		3	304	212
29	9	3	1	6	222	125
30	8				205	
31	31	37	2	4	178	127
32					63	
33				1		44
34	8		1		297	
35						
Total	139	138	34	47	4148	2976

#	1976 Attend at Principal Worship	1982 Attend at Principal Worship	1976 Total Prep Members	1982 Total Prep Members	1976 Church School Members	1982 Church School Members
#	9	9	10	10	11	11
1	20	25	4		52	33
2	175	150	28	27	240	164
3	133	20	18	4	155	25
4		3				3
5		21				21
6		11				16
7						
8	50	61		10	65	79
9	82	116	2		94	125
10	71	84	10	8	99	119
11		65		7		96
12	77	50	9		62	30
13	89		4	25	108	59
14	35	26	30	49	225	155
15						
16						
17						
18						
19						
20	43	63	26	28	77	33
21						
22	6	15			6	10
23		20		7		
24						
25	103	97	74	60	108	84
26						
27						
28	155	63	5	12	130	86
29	57	46	22	21	52	59
30	81		95		139	
31	71	48	31	20	90	46
32	40		3		30	
33		39		16		57
34	125		117		175	
35						
Total:	1413	1023	478	294	1907	1300

#Column	1976 Church School Attend	1982 Church School Attend	1976 UMW Local Work	1982 UMW Local Work	1976 No. Org. Churches	1982 No. Org. Churches
#Column	12	12	13	13	14	14
1	22	30			1	1
2	121	82	550	469	2	2
3	93	18	800		4	1
4						1
5		21				1
6		11				1
7						
8	35	44	270	798	2	2
9	70	96			3	3
10	79	60			3	1
11		65				2
12	30	40	330	300	3	3
13	70		229		2	2
14	112	90	162	432	2	2
15						
16						
17						
18						
19						
20	44	16	363	350	1	1
21						
22	15	6	300		1	1
23				584		1
24						
25	38	13	1349	50	2	2
26						
27						
28	100	49	300	105	3	3
29	25	20	300	169	2	2
30	50		340		2	
31	39	26	761		2	2
32	24		185		1	
33		31		1881		1
34	80		1500		1	
35						
	1047	718	7739	5138	37	35

#Column	1976 Value All Property 15	1982 Value All Property 15	1976 All Debt 16	1982 All Debt 16	1976 Paid on Debt 17	1982 Paid on Debt 17
1	$15,400	$90,000			$191	$5,500
2	$318,400	$715,400	$3,624	$12,341	$6,540	$13,619
3	$90,200	$7,000	$1,500		$13,000	
4		$5,000				
5		$25,000				
6		$7,000				$1,000
7						
8	$96,000	$169,000			$320	$9,367
9	$103,500	$163,850		$1,250		$6,096
10	$63,750	$225,000			$3,427	$2,856
11		$91,800				$10,831
12	$177,200	$16,200			$782	$4,093
13	$22,000	$85,000			$200	$4,830
14	$627,000	$916,385			$1,484	
15						
16						
17						
18						
19						
20	$4,300	$154,175	$3,000		$1,962	
21						
22	$24,500	$37,000				
23		$35,000				
24						
25	$155,000	$16,850	$8,401		$2,232	$2,032
26						
27						
28	$80,000	$104,500				
29	$206,260	$343,000		$2,500	$3,108	$1,261
30	$78,500		$6,554		$1,946	$10,469
31	$214,000	$333,500			$1,948	$938
32	$72,000				$2,300	$6,850
33		$62,431				$2,524
34	$225,000		$26,592		$4,402	$14,036
35						
	$2,573,010	$3,603,091	$49,671	$16,091	$43,842	$96,302

#	1976 All Clergy Expense 21	1982 All Clergy Expense 21	1976 All Connect Expense 22	1982 All Connect Expense 22	1976 World Service & Con.Ben. 23	1982 World Service & Con.Ben 23
#Column21						
1	$244		$45		$148	
2	$11,449	$18,120	$1,130	$2,288	$4,400	$4,032
3	$2,530	$451	$61	$64	$41	$191
4		$5				$25
5		$185		$3		
6		$140		$28		$61
7						
8	$2,160	$4,763	$136	$406	$390	$852
9		$61		$277		$329
10	$1,783	$2,811	$166	$306	$798	$713
11		$431				
12	$2,703	$2,975	$260	$315	$907	$1,000
13	$187	$297	$108	$36	$181	$106
14	$5,568	$15,055	$1,130	$2,083	$1,218	$3,730
15						
16						
17						
18						
19						
20	$3,293	$4,067	$833	$393	$879	$121
21						
22	$16	$327	$17	$114	$18	$129
23		$170		$59		$260
24						
25	$1,458	$7,521	$1,591	$1,052	$1,678	$3,678
26						
27						
28	$2,108	$343	$406	$308	$294	$249
29	$3,695	$6,463		$198	$39	$476
30	$1,886	$5,080	$185	$352	$851	$2,041
31	$3,224	$10,243	$387	$638	$989	$272
32	$476	$5,597	$51	$1,306	$336	$5,089
33		$10,544		$319		$837
34	$4,121	$3,776	$253	$635	$1,526	$3,801
35						
	$46,901	$99,425	$6,759	$11,180	$14,693	$27,992

#	1976 Other Benev.	1982 Other Benev.	1976 UMW funds to denom. Funds	1982 UMW funds to denom. Funds	1976 Grand Total Paid	1982 Grand Total Paid
#Column24	24	25	25	26	26	
1	$61				$1,779	$11,500
2	$12,887	$10,176	$1,719	$2,604	$67,820	$10,337
3	$165	$189	$10		$21,004	$3,107
4		$20				$143
5		$12				$1,975
6		$83				$2,467
7						
8	$133	$1,835	$192		$10,082	$28,002
9	$85	$1,299		$25	$85	$35,342
10	$740	$1,470	$84	$100	$13,749	$22,217
11						$12,342
12	$1,526	$1,579	$108	$574	$15,140	$40,733
13	$92	$70			$2,859	$9,033
14	$7,547	$6,540	$533		$59,330	$68,748
15						
16						
17						
18						
19						
20	$1,848	$352	$343	$159	$23,315	$21,379
21						
22	$58	$58			$2,171	$5,495
23		$75		$35		$1,890
24						
25	$1,629	$2,468	$525	$550	$23,354	$46,657
26						
27						
28	$338	$172	$78		$11,453	$20,291
29	$185	$191	$200		$18,703	$32,579
30	$260	$660	$172	$400	$9,278	$28,765
31	$1,777	$1,081	$83		$21,730	$26,911
32	$410	$1,454		$700	$4,623	$37,341
33		$1,495		$265		$30,827
34	$400	$1,520	$75	$56	$21,967	$36,614
35						
	$30,141	$32,799	$4,122	$5,468	$328,442	$534,695

1989 Lowest Per Capita Counties in Each State

These counties are the lowest for their state in 1989. Also listed are other counties that would be in the project if done for 1989, and counties in the project for 1986 that would have been dropped in 1989.

State	County	Income
Alabama	Lowndes	$4,646
Alaska	Wade Hampton	$4,666
Arizona	Apache	$4,268
Arkansas	Lee	$4,779
California	Imperial	$7,170
Connecticut	Windham	$10,348
Delaware	Kent	$9,284
Florida	Union	$5,630
Georgia	Quitman	$5,431
Hawaii	Kauai	$9,520
Idaho	Owyhee	$4,827
Illinois	Pulaski	$6,559
Indiana	Crawford	$6,929
Iowa	Ringgold	$5,627
Kansas	Wallace	$6,006
Kentucky	Owsley	$4,292
	Elliott	$5,381
	McCreary	$5,390
Louisiana	East Carroll	$4,134
Maine	Washington	$6,929
Maryland	Garrett	$7,406
Massachusetts	Bristol	$9,961
Michigan	Ogemaw	$6,490
Minnesota	Red Lake	$6,182
Mississippi	Tunica	$4,042
	Jefferson	$4,987
Missouri	Shannon	$5,659
Montana	Petroleum	$2,974
Nebraska	Logan	$2,209
	Arthur	$2,312
	Keya Paha	$2,635
	Banner	$3,227
	Rock	$3,274
	Sioux	$3,321
	Loup	$3,600
	Blaine	$3,619
	Hayes	$3,692
	McPherson	$4,000
Nevada	Eureka	$6,450
New Jersey	Cumberland	$9,137
New Mexico	McKinley	$4,743
	Mora	$4,821
New York	Allegany	$7,532
North Carolina	Twain	$5,791
North Dakota	Sioux	$4,138

Ohio	Adams.	$6,447
Oregon	Malheur.	$7,142
Pennsylvania	Potter.	$6,964
Rhode Island	Providence.	$10,335
South Carolina	Dillon.	$5,855
South Dakota	Shannon.	$3,419
	Ziebach..	$3,392
	Dewey..	$3,430
	Buffalo.	$3,572
	Corson.	$3,677
	Jackson..	$3,683
	Harding..	$3,978
Tennessee	Hancock.	$4,274
Texas	Starr.	$3,312
	Maverick.	$3,892
	Zavala..	$4,802
Utah	San Juan..	$4,384
Vermont	Essex.	$7,472
Virginia	Lee..	$6,437
Washington	Ferry..	$7,054
West Virginia	Clay.	$4,840
Wisconsin Menominee..		$4,857
Wyoming Niobara..		$6,749

Certainly, the lowest ranking income counties for any given year will comprise a different list.

Lowest Per Capita Income 2008 Prepared from Census and Wikipedia

	County	State	County Seat	Per Capita Income	Support
1	Buffalo	SD	GannValley	$5,213.00	
2	Shannon	SD	Pine Ridge	$6,286.00	
3	Starr	TX	Rio Grande City	$7,069.00	
4	Ziebach	SD	Dupree	$7,463.00	
5	Todd	SD	Mission	$7,714.00	
6	Sioux	ND	Fort Yates	$7,731.00	
7	Corson	SD	McLaughlin	$8,615.00	
8	Wade Hampton	AK	Hooper Bay	$8,717.00	
9	Maverick	TX	Eagle Pass	$8,758.00	
10	Apache	AZ	St Johns	$8,986.00	
11	Dewey	SD	Timber Lake	$8,251.00	
12	Willacy	TX	Raymondville	$9,421.00	
13	Hudspeth	TX	Sierra Blanca	$9,549.00	
14	Presidio	TX	Marfa	$9,558.00	
15	East Carroll Parish	LA	Lk Providence	$9,629.00	
16	La Salle	TX	Cotulla	$9,692.00	
17	Jefferson	MS	Fayette	$9,709.00	
18	Clay	KY	Manchester	$9,716.00	
19	Dimmitt	TX	Carrizo Springs	$9,765.00	
20	McKinley	NM	Grants	$9,872.00	
21	McCreary	KY	Pine Knot	$9,876.00	
22	Hidalgo	TX	MacAllen	$9,899.00	
23	Jackson	SD	Kadoka	$9,981.00	
24	Zavala	TX	Crystal City	$10,034.00	
25	Bennett	SD	Martin	$10,106.00	
26	Madison Parish	LA	Tallulah	$10,114.00	
27	Bullock	AL	Union Springs	$10,163.00	
28	McDowell	WV	Welch	$10,174.00	
29	San Juan	UT	Monticello	$10,229.00	
30	Brooks	TX	Falfurrias	$10,234.00	
31	Wolfe	KY	Campton	$10,321.00	
32	Mellette	SD	White River	$10,362.00	
33	Leslie	KY	Hyden	$10,429.00	

34	Zapata	TX	Zapata	$10,486.00	
35	Hamilton	FL	Jasper	$10,562.00	
36	Issaquena	MS	Valley Park	$10,581.00	
37	Bee	TX	Beeville	$10,525.00	
38	Menominee	WI	Keshena	$10,625.00	
39	Martin	KY	Lovely	$10,650.00	
40	Knox	KY	Heidrick	$10,660.00	
41	Holmes	MS	Lexington	$10,683.00	
42	Magoffin	KY	Fredville	$10,685.00	
43	Jackson	KY	McKee	$10,711.00	
44	Owsley	KY	Booneville	$10,742.00	
45	Costilla	CO	San Luis	$10,748.00	
46	Tallahatchie	MS	Charleston	$10,749.00	
47	Webb	TX	Laredo	$10,759.00	
48	Big Horn	MT	Prior	$10,792.00	
49	Lake	TN	Tiptonville	$10,794.00	
50	Reeves	TX	Pecos	$10,811.00	
51	Quitman	MS	Marks	$10,817.00	
52	Wilkinson	MS	Woodville	$10,868.00	
53	Rolette	ND	Belcourt	$10,873.00	
54	Wilcox	AL	Camden	$10,903.00	
55	Hancock	GA	Sparta	$10,916.00	
56	Humphreys	MS	Belzoni	$10,926.00	
57	Perry	AL	Marion	$10,948.00	
58	Thurston	NE	Winnebago	$10,951.00	
59	Madison	ID	Rexburg	$10,956.00	
60	Cameron	TX	Brownsville	$10,960.00	
61	Lee	AR	Marianna	$10,983.00	
62	Breathitt	KY	Guage	$11,044.00	
63	Clark	ID	Dubois	$11,141.00	
64	Adair	OK	Stillwell	$11,185.00	
65	Luna	NM	Deming	$11,218.00	
66	Guadalupe	NM	Santa Rosa	$11,241.00	
67	Claiborne	MS	Port Gibson	$11,244.00	
68	Allendale	SC	Allendale	$11,293.00	
69	Knott	KY	Vicco	$11,297.00	

70	Duval	TX	San Diego	$11,324.00	
71	Roosevelt	MT	Wolf Point	$11,347.00	
72	Sunflower	MS	Indianola	$11,365.00	
73	Sharkey	MS	Rolling Fork	$11,396.00	
74	Menifee	KY	Frenchburg	$11,399.00	
75	Evangeline Parish	LA	Ville Platte	$11,432.00	
76	Sumter	AL	Livingston	$11,491.00	
77	Calhoun	WV	Grantsville	$11,491.00	
78	Shannon	MO	Winona	$11,492.00	
79	Culbertson	TX	Van Horn	$11,493.00	
80	Charles Mix	SD	Geddes	$11,502.00	
81	Benson	ND	Leeds	$11,509.00	
82	Bell	KY	Middlesboro	$11,526.00	
83	Harlan	KY	Cumberland	$11,585.00	
84	Glacier	MT	Browning	$11,597.00	
85	Navajo	AZ	Winslow	$11,609.00	
86	Cibola	NM	Gallup	$11,731.00	
87	Winn Parish	LA	Winnfield	$11,794.00	
88	Randolph	GA	Cuthbert	$11,809.00	
89	Macon	GA	Marshallville	$11,820.00	
90	Calhoun	GA	Morgan	$11,839.00	
91	Keya Paha	NE	Springview	$11,860.00	
92	Greene	MS	Leakesville	$11,868.00	
93	Wheatland	MT	Harlowton	$11,954.00	
94	Concordia Parish	LA	Monteray	$11,966.00	
95	Jefferson Davis	MS	Prentiss	$11,974.00	
96	Tunica	MS	Tunica	$11,978.00	
97	Letcher	KY	Whitesburg	$11,984.00	
98	Kemper	MS	De Kalb	$11,985.00	
99	Hancock	TN	Sneedville	$11,986.00	
100	Lawrence	KY	Adams	$12,008.00	

www.ingramcontent.com/pod-product-compliance
Lightning Source LLC
Chambersburg PA
CBHW081351280526
45788CB00009B/2847